THE 10 RULES OF SUCCESSFUL NATIONS

Also by Ruchir Sharma

The Rise and Fall of Nations:
Forces of Change in the Post-Crisis World

Breakout Nations:
In Pursuit of the Next Economic Miracles

THE

10

RULES OF

SUCCESSFUL

NATIONS

RUCHIR SHARMA

W. W. NORTON & COMPANY

Independent Publishers Since 1923

For information about special discounts for bulk purchases, please contact W. W. Norton Special Sales at specialsales@wwnorton.com or 800-233-4830

Manufacturing by Lake Book Manufacturing
Book design by Daniel Lagin
Production manager: Julia Druskin

ISBN 978-0-393-65194-2

W. W. Norton & Company, Inc., 500 Fifth Avenue, New York, N.Y. 10110
www.wwnorton.com

W. W. Norton & Company Ltd., 15 Carlisle Street, London W1D 3BS

1 2 3 4 5 6 7 8 9 0

CONTENTS

THE 10 RULES OF
SUCCESSFUL NATIONS

Introduction

IMPERMANENCE

Economists have failed to predict every US recession since records began, including the Great Recession that rattled the world in 2008. They are under attack even within their own ranks for being too academic—too focused on elegant mathematical models that pretend humans always act rationally, or on data that is updated too infrequently to foretell big economic shifts.

Everyone knows that forecasting is a mug's game, but also necessary and unavoidable. Politicians, technocrats, businesspeople, and investors all have a huge stake in predicting the economic rise and fall of nations, since they can't begin to formulate plans or policies without making an educated estimate as to what is coming next. Getting it right can help billions of people; the costs of getting it wrong are equally large.

This book, culled from my quarter century in the game, outlines ten rules for spotting whether a country is on the rise, on the decline, or just muddling through. Together, the rules work as a system for spotting change.

1

A few basic principles underlie all the rules. The first is to recognize the impermanence of economic trends and the regular rhythms of change. Recent crises are just the latest reminder that the normal condition of the world is impermanence—an environment prone to booms, busts, and protests.

In the 1960s the fast-growing Philippine economy was being feted as the future of Asia, and that buzz helped Manila win the right to host the headquarters of the Asian Development Bank. By the next decade, under the dictatorship of Ferdinand Marcos, growth was stalling, but the ADB was in Manila for good. In the 1970s, similar exercises in extrapolation led some American scholars and intelligence analysts to predict that the Soviet economy was destined to become the largest in the world. Instead, it collapsed at the end of the 1980s.

Hard experience did not prevent a new outburst of hype in the first decade of the twenty-first century, when global forces—easy money pouring out of Western banks, spiking prices of commodities, and soaring global trade—doubled the growth rate of emerging nations. By 2007, the number of economies expanding faster than 5 percent had reached 100, or five times the postwar norm—but forecasters assumed this freak event was a lasting condition. They figured that if the hot economies stayed hot, the average incomes of many emerging nations would soon catch up to, or "converge" with, those of rich nations. Envisioning a world without poor countries was about as plausible as forecasting a world without poor people, but few questioned these forecasts.

Marketers had started calling Brazil, Russia, India, and China the "BRICs" to capture the idea that these emerging giants were a solid bet to dominate the global economy. They assumed China's rise would lift up countries like Russia and Brazil, which had been thriving mainly by exporting oil and other commodities to the Chinese. Ever-growing demand from China would drive a "super cycle" of rising commodity prices and growing wealth from Moscow to Lagos. At the same time, global trade and capital flows were soaring, and many forecasters thought those forces would help boost incomes in the big emerging markets.

This optimism was derailed by the crisis of 2008. Trade flows slowed. Money flows collapsed. The price of oil and other commodities fell sharply, and by 2014, analysts were spoofing the BRICs as "broken," crumbling, and a "bloody ridiculous investment concept."[1] Since then China's annual GDP growth has slumped from 14 to 6 percent, and less by private estimates.[2] As of 2019, Russia and Brazil were growing at 1 percent. India, the one BRIC that looked reasonably solid in 2014, was slowing sharply as well.

The fate of the BRICs is a reminder that it is hard to sustain rapid economic growth. The widespread prosperity of the West after World War II, and across the world after 1980, has blinded many to this fact. Looking back 150 years, researchers at Goldman Sachs found dozens of "great stagnations," long slumps that lowered a nation's average income, relative to its peers. Of these slumps, 90 lasted at least six years, and 26 spanned more than ten years. These slumps hit countries ranging from Germany in the 1860s and '70s to France in the first decade of the twenty-first century. The longest lasted twenty-three years and struck India starting in 1930. Even before the Industrial Revolution, major regions of Europe and Asia went through phases stretching hundreds of years with virtually no growth.[3]

Writers have lavished attention on the post–World War II "miracles"—particularly Asian nations like Japan, South Korea, and Taiwan—that sustained strong growth for decades and graduated from the developing to the developed ranks. But they are rare exceptions to the rule of impermanence. The long slumps and extended setbacks are more common, and at least as relevant as the postwar "miracles" to understanding how economies really work. Yet forecasters have continued to assume that booms—from China to India and Kenya—will last indefinitely. The impermanence of economic conditions means that one can never extrapolate current trends into the distant future.

Keep the Future Close

One basic goal of this book is to refocus economic conversation on a practical time frame. Trends in globalization have ebbed and flowed since at least the twelfth century, when Genghis Khan secured commerce along the Silk Road, and the cycles of business, technology, and politics that shape economic growth are short, typically about five years. As a result, any forecast that looks beyond the next cycle or two—five to ten years—is likely to be way off the mark.

Predictions that look 20 to 100 years into the future cannot possibly survive change in the intervening years. New economic competitors can arise, as China did in the early 1980s, or as eastern Europe did in the 1990s. New technology can emerge, as the internet did in the 1990s and as new digital manufacturing techniques like 3-D printing are doing now. When a country like Japan, China, or India grows rapidly for a decade, analysts should be looking not for reasons the streak will continue but for the moment the cycle will turn.

For practical people, forecasting is all about timing. The dogged consistency of permabulls and permabears undermines their credibility, because timing matters. Economists like Nouriel Roubini, who had been predicting a US debt meltdown for many years, were given a lot of credit when it finally came in 2008. But had businesses, policy-makers, and investors built plans around those warnings, they would have missed the global boom before 2008 and all the opportunities that came with it. Practical forecasters focus on dynamic indicators that can reveal critical change at the margin, meaning imminent shifts in the economy that can foretell its basic direction for the next five years. They ignore futurists predicting the coming Asian or African century.

Noted psychologist Philip Tetlock has put thousands of predictions to the test, and in his book *Superforecasting*[4] he presents evidence confirming that forecasts get less reliable the farther they reach into the future, and that they become no more accurate than random guesses beyond five years.

The Market as Mirror

A realistic approach to economic forecasting also needs to weed out data that is not forward-looking, reliable, and up to date. In early 2014, Nigeria revised its official GDP to $500 billion, almost doubling the size of the economy. This transformation caused no stir because people who watch emerging markets have grown accustomed to shifting numbers. Commenting on the frequent revision of official Indian economic data, former central bank governor Y. V. Reddy once cracked to me that while the future is always uncertain, in India even the past is uncertain.

Numbers coming out of the emerging world have a way of morphing to satisfy the interests of major players. In China, skeptical analysts have started checking official GDP growth figures against data they consider more reliable, such as electricity consumption. In 2015, however, reports emerged that the government was instructing developers to keep the lights on even in empty apartment complexes—so that electricity consumption data would confirm official growth numbers. Four years later, the informal data still suggested that the official growth claims were too high.

Investors take pains to find real-time intelligence from the field, and market movements accurately reflect their collective wisdom about the prospects of an economy. True, markets are subject to flights of panic, and critics like to quote Nobel Prize–winning economist Paul Samuelson, who quipped in 1966 that the stock market had "predicted nine out of the last five recessions." But Samuelson was no more impressed by economists, who have a worse forecasting record than markets. Ned Davis Research has shown that "economists, as a consensus, called exactly none" of the last seven recessions, dating back to 1970.[5] In the United States, the National Bureau of Economic Research is the official documenter of recessions, and on average it has recognized the start of recessions eight months *after* the beginning of the recession.

To see how well markets anticipate trouble for the economy, I looked at data for the past fifty years for periods when the S&P 500 fell from its most recent peak by 10, 15, or 20 percent. It turned out that, typically, the market declined by at least 15 percent six months before the seven US recessions officially began. In short, the market sniffed out trouble in a timely manner.

But, as Samuelson suggested, the stock market also raised false alarms. The S&P 500 has suffered 15 percent declines twelve times since 1965, so there were five times when a sharp decline was not followed by a recession, most recently in 2011. All told, though, the market accurately signaled a coming recession 60 percent of the time. Economists as a group got it right zero percent of the time.

Credit and commodity markets can also be timely indicators. In financial circles, copper is known as "Dr. Copper" because a sharp decline in its price is almost always an ominous sign for the global economy. In the United States, one of few countries where most lending is done through bonds and other credit market products rather than through banks, the credit markets started sending distress signals well before the onset of the last three recessions, in 1990, 2001, and 2007. The credit markets also send false signals on occasion, but for the most part they have been a fairly reliable bellwether.

Stifle Biases

The prosperity of the postwar era created what World Bank researchers have called "optimism bias," a tendency to predict that strong growth streaks will continue and weak economies will soon revive. After a shock like the global financial crisis in 2008, however, the popular mood was likely to revert to pessimism, which Austrian-born economist Joseph Schumpeter described as the default attitude of the intellectual classes. The trick for forecasters is not to get caught up in the current mood, and to remember the widely known but widely ignored tendency of any economic trend (whether in GDP, investment, credit, or other factors) to regress to the mean—or return to its long-term average.

The tendency to believe that current trends will endure is magnified by "anchoring bias." Conversations tend to build on the point that starts or anchors them. During the first decade of this century, the average growth rate of emerging nations accelerated to the unprecedented rate of 7 percent, and economists came to see 7 percent as the new standard. By 2010, the notion that emerging economies were about to see growth drop to 4 percent seemed implausibly pessimistic, even though 4 percent is their average growth rate in the postwar era. Yet that drop is what happened.

In general, the correct anchor for any forecast is as far back as solid data exists, the better to grasp the historic pattern. The patterns of boom and bust described in this book are based on my own research, including a database of postwar emerging economies that managed to grow at a rate of 6 percent for at least a decade. Though many emerging economies still aspire to grow faster, few do. Six percent is rapid enough to lift their average incomes eventually to developed world levels, yet moderate enough that it yields a broad and statistically significant sample of fifty-six cases.[*]

The habit of hanging on to an improbable anchor is com-

---

[*] See the Appendix for this list of fifty-six postwar success stories.

pounded by "confirmation bias," the tendency to collect only data that confirms one's existing beliefs. In the first ten years of this century, hype for the BRICS dominated public discussions. Liberal advocates for the poor were thrilled by the rise of poor nations; investors on Wall Street were thrilled by the prospect of making fortunes in the big emerging markets. Many found data to confirm the hype. Few wanted to hear that it was all likely soon to revert to the mean. But it did.

The question to ask is never, *What will the world look like if current trends hold?* It is, rather, *What will happen if the normal pattern holds and cycles continue to turn?* In a sense, the rules are all about playing the right probabilities, based on the cyclical patterns of an impermanent world.

What Matters Most

Often, economists and writers oversell the importance of a single factor—geographic location, the "curse of oil," the advantage of liberal institutions or of a young and growing population—as the key to understanding what makes nations succeed or fail. These factors are often important in shaping growth, and my rules take account of all of them. But no single factor determines how an economy is likely to change over the next five years. For example, the "curse of oil" is real: many countries have grown poorer since they discovered oil, owing to the corruption that often bubbles up around hydrocarbons. But a gut distaste for unsavory petrostates can blind forecasters to the likelihood that when global oil prices enter a boom decade, many oil economies will follow.

On the other hand, sprawling, multidimensional growth models are even more common. Most forecasters understand that economic growth is the product of multiple factors, and the balance of these factors will shift over time, as a country grows richer and as global conditions change. Institutions such as the World Bank and the International Monetary Fund count hundreds of factors that have an impact on growth, from the share of university students who are studying law to whether the country in question is a former Spanish colony.

Trying to avoid the mistakes of excessive simplicity and unmanageable complexity, I settled on a system of ten rules—enough to capture the big picture without bogging down in detail. The rules emerged from my twenty-five years of experience leading a team of investors in emerging markets, and trying to make sense of the fascinating welter of data and observations they would pick up on the road. Early on, the discussions tended to wander with the whims of the person in the field. So we started to test our observations empirically, to see which ones really worked in forecasting. The rules distill that research, narrowing down the thousands of factors that can determine the economic success of nations to the ten that matter most.

One way to think about economic growth is that it is the sum of population growth and productivity growth: how many more workers are entering the labor force, plus how much more they are producing. Throughout recorded economic history, in fact, population has accounted for half of GDP growth. That is why the first chapter focuses on the inexorable impact of population trends on the economy, and what governments can do about it. In a way, this is half the story.

The rest of the rules deal one way or another with the other half of the growth story, which is captured in a loose way by the productivity growth numbers. Between 1960 and 2005, the average annual productivity growth rate worldwide was around 2 percent, but that rate downshifted by almost a full percentage point in the last ten years. Like population growth rates, productivity growth rates have fallen by varying degrees, from less than a percentage point in the United States to more than 2 points in South Korea and nearly 4 points in Greece.

The big difference is that population growth is easy to measure, and there is no question about the scale of the slowdown. Productivity is very hard to measure, and debate rages about whether the productivity decline is real. Optimists say existing measures fail to capture the cost and time savings produced by new technologies, including robots, artificial intelligence, and the "internet of things." Skeptics say these new technologies contribute as much to wasting time—on gaming, cat videos, and the like—as to boosting productivity.

Whichever side is right, population data is reliable, and is therefore a very practical economic forecasting tool. Productivity data is too fuzzy to be useful in itself, so the rest of my rules get at this side of the story in other ways.

Economic growth can also be thought about as the sum of spending by government, spending by consumers, and investment to build factories or homes and businesses. Of these, investment is by far the most important generator and indicator of change, because investment generates the income that makes spending by government and consumers possible.

Growth can also be broken down by the major sectors: agriculture, services, and manufacturing. Of these, manufacturing has the biggest impact on the direction of the economy, because it has traditionally been the main source of jobs, innovation, and increases in productivity. So the rules have a lot to say about investment and about factories, but much less to say about consumers and farmers.

Similarly, when the rules drill down into investment and manufacturing, or currencies and debt, they aim to narrow the hundreds of measures one could use to track these factors to the one or two that matter most. To anticipate the next global financial crisis, which among thousands of available debt measurements should we be watching?

For the purpose of forecasting, it's also important, perhaps counterintuitively, to ignore long-term factors that economists and politicians may love, but that don't work well as signs of change. The payoff from investment in education, for example, is so slow and variable that it is almost useless as a predictor of economic change in the foreseeable future. The Soviet-era legacy of excellence in education has given Russia the highest average number of years of schooling (11.5) and the largest share of university grads (6.4 percent) of any emerging economy, but with little impact on economic growth. In China, the economy took off in the 1980s as officials lavished money on roads, factories, and other investments that had a fast impact on growth; good schools came later. The post–World War

II booms in the United States and Britain have often been linked to the spread of public education, but that change began before World War I. So my rules largely ignore the sacrosanct subject of schools.

Aspiring to scientific credibility, economists also tend to ignore any factor that is too soft to quantify or incorporate into a forecasting model—even a factor as critical as politics. Numbers alone can't capture the impact of an energetic new leader bent on economic reform or, on the flip side, lining his cronies' pockets. My rules therefore offer a mix of ways to read hard data on critical factors like credit, prices, and money flows, as well as softer signs of shifts in leadership and policy.

An Eye for Balance

Emerging countries often grow in torrid streaks, only to fall into major crises that wipe out all their gains. That's why among the nearly 200 economies currently tracked by the IMF, only 40 have reached the "developed" class. The last to make it was South Korea, two decades ago. The rest are emerging, and most have been emerging forever. All the rules aim, one way or another, to capture the delicate balances of debt, investment, inflation, currency values, and other key factors required to keep an economy growing steadily faster than its peers.

These are the basic principles: Remember that economic trends are impermanent; churn and crisis are the norm. Avoid straight-line forecasting, foggy discussions of the coming century, and sweeping single-factor theories. Stifle biases, whether political, cultural, or "anchoring." Recognize that any economy, no matter how successful or how broken, is more likely to return to the long-term average growth rate for its income class than to remain abnormally hot or cold indefinitely. Watch for balanced growth, and focus on a manageable set of dynamic indicators that make it possible to anticipate turns in the cycle. With these principles in mind, the rules can help turn the "dismal science" into a practical art, and perhaps nudge economists to think in ways that could help anticipate the next big crisis.

1

POPULATION

Successful Nations Fight Demographic Decline

The impact of population growth on the economy is very straight-forward, and very large. If more workers are entering the labor force, they boost the economy's potential to grow, while fewer will diminish that potential. And unlike any other major force in economics, population growth is a function of just a few factors—fertility, longevity, and immigration—which can be measured with high accuracy. The result is that the track record of population forecasts is strikingly good. Starting in the 1950s, the United Nations issued forecasts for global population in the year 2000 a total of twelve times, and all but one of those forecasts was off by less than 4 percent.

According to numbers from the authoritative Maddison data-base, going back more than 1,000 years, the world economy has never broken free of the limits imposed by population growth. Throughout, increases in population have accounted for roughly half of economic growth. Before the Industrial Revolution of the late nineteenth century, annual global population growth did not exceed half a percent, and global economic growth did not exceed 1 percent—for any sustained period. Population growth increased to 1 percent by the early part of the twentieth century, on the back of falling mortality rates, and economic growth accelerated to about 2 percent. After World War II, the baby boom pushed population growth toward 2 percent, and economic growth rose to an annual pace of nearly 4 percent for the first and only time in history.

Then came a stark shift. As emerging countries like China started to implement strict birth control policies, and women in developed countries started to delay or avoid childbirth to pursue careers, suddenly around 1990 population growth started to dry up. Fears of overpopulation, which had wracked the world in the 1960s and '70s, began to fade. Fifteen years later, the growth rate in the world's working-age population—defined as people between the ages of 15 and 64—also began to fall sharply.

Today, successful nations are taking aggressive steps to combat working-age population decline. To identify those countries, look first at the natural growth rate in that age group. This rate is a baseline for how fast an economy can grow. A 1 percent decline in the working-age population growth rate will shave about 1 percentage point off economic growth, which is roughly the story of the last fifteen years.

In the five decades before 2005, growth in the global working-age population had averaged 1.9 percent a year, but it has since plummeted to 1.2 percent. Nonetheless, most economists have yet to lower their economic growth forecasts accordingly. One reason is "anchoring bias": 4 percent global economic growth has been the norm for much of their lifetimes, and their assumptions are still anchored in that era. Another is that, by sheer coincidence, the collapse in working-age population growth came on the eve of the global financial crisis, which became the go-to explanation for all the world economy's ills.

The economic impact of the demographic downshift is hard to overstate: if population growth had stayed around 2 percent—the trend rate between 1950 and 2005—the global population today would be 8.7 billion, not 7.7 billion. And very few countries would be worried about the new demographic drag on economic growth.

The working-age population is already shrinking in Germany and China; it is growing, but very slowly, in the United States; and it is booming in only a handful of large emerging countries, including Nigeria, the Philippines, and Saudi Arabia. The United Nations forecasts that population growth will continue slowing through the end of this century, all over the world.

Next, look at what governments are doing to counteract slow population growth. One tactic is financial "bonuses" for women to have more children, but these incentives have a spotty record and are not a promising sign over a practical time frame, since it takes at least fifteen years for newborns to age into the labor force.

Governments can, however, quickly address the demographic challenge by tapping often underutilized pools of adult labor. In particular, they can increase the size of the labor force by encouraging immigrants, women, and retirees to enter or reenter the job market. Perhaps most controversially, they can subsidize robots in the workforce.

The 2 Percent Population Pace Test

Unlike most of my rules, demographics are not a dynamic indicator of coming shifts. The number of young adults entering the workforce changes glacially, but it sets a baseline for how fast the economy can grow and is therefore too important to ignore.

Consider my database of the fifty-six postwar cases in which a country sustained an average economic growth rate of 6 percent or more for at least a decade. In three out of every four, from Brazil in the 1960s to Malaysia in the 1990s, the working-age population grew at an average pace of at least 2 percent a year. In short, if a country's working-age population growth rate is not above 2 percent, the country is not likely to enjoy a long economic boom.

Moreover, when economies did boom without 2 percent population growth, they did so in unusual circumstances. Some, like Japan in the 1960s or Russia after the fall of Communism, were rebuilding after a period of war or crisis. Others were already relatively well off, such as Chile and Ireland in the 1990s, when reform and new investment increased productivity and compensated for weak population growth.

The 2 percent pace test does not bode well for the world's growth prospects. In the 1980s, seventeen of the twenty largest emerging economies had a working-age population growth rate above 2 percent, but after 2010 that number fell to just two: Nigeria and Saudi Arabia. It is expected to fall to just one—Nigeria—after 2020. The number of working-age people is also growing at a rate near or above 2 percent in some smaller economies, such as Kenya, Pakistan, and Bangladesh. But the overall picture is clear:

a world with fewer booming populations will produce fewer economic stars.

The Uncertain Demographic Dividend

Even in countries with strong population growth, leaders need to avoid falling for the idea that population booms pay off automatically in rapid economic growth.

Before 2000, strong population growth was common but typically did not produce an economic boom. Scanning the record for nearly 200 countries, going back to 1960, I found 698 cases in which data for both population growth and GDP growth are available for a full decade. In more than 60 percent of these cases, the country had a working-age population growth rate of more than 2 percent, but only a quarter of those population booms were accompanied by average GDP growth of 6 percent or more. The countries where a population boom failed to produce rapid economic growth include Turkey in every decade between 1960 and 2000, and the Philippines between 1960 and 2010.

Good demographics are often a necessary condition for rapid growth, but never a sufficient condition. The "dividend" pays off only if political leaders create the environment necessary to attract investment and generate jobs.

In the 1960s and '70s, booming populations in Africa, China, and India led to famines, unemployment, and civil strife. In the Arab world, the working-age population grew by 3 percent a year between 1985 and 2005, with no economic dividend. By 2010, high youth unemployment was fueling discontent from Iraq to Tunisia, where the Arab Spring revolts began the next year. India, too, had assumed that its booming population would provide a demographic dividend, but now it struggles to generate jobs for all its youth. So, look at the working-age population growth rate to understand the economy's potential, then look at what the government is doing to realize that potential.

When Populations Shrink

If the population is shrinking, it is close to impossible to generate strong economic growth, or as the European Commission warned in 2005, "Never in history has there been economic growth without population growth."[1]

In my analysis of population and GDP growth in 200 countries going back to 1960, I found only 38 cases (out of 698) in which the working-age population was shrinking over the course of a decade. The average GDP growth rate in these cases was just 1.5 percent; only 3 of these countries managed to sustain a GDP growth rate of 6 percent or more. All three were small countries in special circumstances: Portugal after opening to free trade in the 1960s, and Georgia and Belarus following the tumultuous collapse of the Soviet Union.

This record suggests that rapid GDP growth is unlikely in countries with shrinking populations, which are increasingly common. In the early 1980s, there were two countries with a declining population of working-age people: war-torn Syria and Afghanistan. In 2019, there were forty-six, including major powers such as China

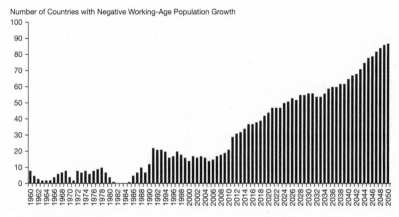

Shrinking Labor Forces

Number of Countries with Negative Working-Age Population Growth

Source: United Nations.

and Russia, and that number is on track to double by the middle of the century.

In China, the working-age population growth rate hovered near 2 percent as recently as 2003, then dropped steadily until it turned negative for the first time in 2015. That makes it unlikely that China can achieve its official growth target of better than 6 percent, and helps explain why 2015 was also the year when China replaced its one-child policy with a two-child policy. The impact of these restrictions will linger, however; China's labor force is still expected to lose a million workers a year in coming years.

Shrinking workforces are the result of falling birth rates. Since 1960, the average number of births per woman has fallen from 4.9 to 2.5 worldwide. In emerging nations, the collapse has been more dramatic, owing in part to those aggressive birth control policies. Fertility rates in India and Mexico have plummeted, from more than 6 in 1960 to nearly 2.1—the "replacement rate" below which the population eventually starts shrinking. Nearly one of every two people on earth already lives in one of eighty-three countries where the birth rate is below the replacement level, including China, Russia, Iran, Brazil, Germany, Japan, and the United States.[2]

Population forecasts also bode poorly for economic growth in developed countries between 2020 and 2025. Among the ten largest developed economies, the number of working-age people is expected to grow at a rate of about 0.2 percent in the United States, Britain, and Canada; shrink a little in France and Spain; and contract at a pace of 0.4 percent a year or more in Italy, Germany, and Japan. The best news for developed countries is confined to smaller ones, led by Singapore and Australia. In short, slower population growth also reduces the potential for powerful economic engines to appear in the developed world.

Baby Bonuses

The race to fight the baby bust is already on. According to the United Nations, 70 percent of developed countries today have implemented policies to boost their fertility rate, up from about 30 percent in 1996. Many nations have tried offering women "baby bonuses," a form of state meddling in the reproductive process that is often controversial, and rarely effective.

In 1987, Singapore pioneered these campaigns, under the slogan "Have three, or more if you can afford it." The incentives it offered, including subsidized hospital stays, had little effect on fertility rate.

Canada introduced a baby bonus in 1988 but later withdrew it, in part because—as other countries have also found—many of the women who responded to direct cash incentives were very poor, and their children added greatly to welfare expenses.[3]

When Australia's treasurer Peter Costello announced baby bonuses in 2005, he urged women to "lie back and think of the aging population,"[4] but they mostly ignored the call, and six years later the government cut the bonuses. Few people struggling to balance career and family are going to respond to officials issuing patriotic calls for more babies.

In France, the socialist government of Prime Minister Lionel Jospin, who was in power from 1997 to 2002, tried to widen the appeal of baby bonuses by making them more generous. Looking to push French fertility back above the replacement rate, it offered lavish incentives for parents having a third child: home-help subsidies, tax cuts, and a 10 percent pension increase, a 75 percent discount on rail tickets, a monthly allowance of over $400. Architects of the plan called baby bonuses "spending on the future," and they are still in place.

Like China's now abandoned one-child policy, baby bonuses are a form of meddling with reproduction and are liable to produce new distortions. In Europe, as demographers Hans-Peter Kohler and Thomas Anderson have argued, the birth rate has fallen especially fast in countries like Germany, where more traditional cultures frowned on mothers returning to work and, as a result, more professional women chose not to have children. In part because of such cultural differences, the impact of state intervention in the human reproductive process is likely to be both slow and unpredictable. The more promising approach is to open doors to adults who are ready and willing to work immediately.

The Battle to Attract Migrants

Every nation prefers to think of itself as productive in the sense of innovative and smart, not just fertile. But population growth—the race to make babies and attract immigrant workers—is where the real action is.

In recent years, productivity growth has not only been slowing across the world; it has also been converging. Looking at the United States, Germany, Japan, Canada, Australia, and Britain, I found that regardless of which two countries you compare, the gap in productivity growth has been narrowing sharply. The reasons are complex, possibly having to do with the accelerating pace at which technology spreads, but if the hotly debated productivity data is accurately capturing the trends, the implication is striking.

For example, the success of the United States, which is often cast as more dynamic than its rivals, owes more to babies and immigrants than to big ideas coming out of Silicon Valley. Until around 2010, for example, productivity was growing significantly faster in the United States than in Japan or Germany, but that advantage has largely disappeared since then. If it weren't for the boost the United States gets from babies and immigrants, its economy would have grown no faster than those of Japan and Europe in the 2010s. In terms of per capita income, the yearly growth rates of the United

States, Germany, the rest of Europe, and Japan have been essentially the same: about half a percentage point.

Therefore, population growth gaps will be increasingly decisive for economic competition. In the battle to attract immigrants, the big winners are expected to include Canada, the United States, and especially Australia, where net migration was on track to increase the population by about 3 percent between 2015 and 2020—the most of any large developed country. Though its population is starting to age, as so many are, the economic impact will be relatively light in Australia—if it keeps its doors open.

That's a big if, given the scale of the anti-immigrant backlash. In 2014 and 2015, a flood of refugees boosted migration into Germany more than eightfold, to over a million a year, triggering street protests. Ultimately, those protests made more open immigration policies politically untenable, even though in theory, Germany could have used every one of the new arrivals, and then some. By my calculation, Germany would have to accept 1.5 million immigrants a year, every year between 2015 and 2030, to maintain its current balance of working-age people to retirees.

But it makes no sense to calculate the immigrant impact on an economy without factoring in the likelihood of political resistance. In Japan, less than 2 percent of the population is foreign-born, compared to 30 percent of Australia's population, and political leaders have only recently begun to question the old assumption that Japan's ethnically "harmonious" culture is an economic advantage. Recognizing the need for more workers, Prime Minister Shinzo Abe increased the number of visas available to economic immigrants after taking power in 2012. The numbers picked up a bit, but Japan would have to increase net migration tenfold—from the current rate of 50,000 people a year—to make up for its projected population decline through 2030. In other words, Japan would have to become another Australia, which is politically improbable.

South Korea, another aging nation that once celebrated its ethnic homogeneity, is more open to change. After the crisis of 1997–98, South Korea began promoting multiculturalism and extending work permits to foreigners in industries facing labor shortages. Since the year 2000, the immigrant population has increased 400 percent, to 1.3 million, compared to an increase of just 50 percent in Japan. Though the working-age population is already shrinking, it would have been shrinking four times more rapidly without the influx of migrants.

Free the Forced Retirees

The next pool of mature labor is the elderly. To figure out which economies are most vulnerable to aging, compare the number of working-age people to the number of people who are older than 64 or younger than 15—also known as the "dependency ratio." When the dependency ratio is rising, fewer workers are available to support the growing number of retirees, and growth suffers.

Dependency ratios are expected to rise especially fast in emerging economies, because of a sharper fall in fertility rates and a faster rise in life expectancy. Worldwide, the average life span is nineteen years longer today than it was in 1960, but in China the average person lives thirty years longer, until the age of 75. This progress has a cost. The share of the Chinese population that is over 65 is on track to double, from 7 to 14 percent, between 2000 and 2027—a period of 28 years. In contrast, that doubling took 115 years in France and 69 years in the United States.

Aging trends impact an economy mainly by increasing or decreasing the number of available workers, but they also impact productivity. In recent years, countries where the dependency ratio is declining also tended to exhibit faster productivity growth. The greater the share of the population that is employed and saving money, the greater the pool of capital, which can be used to invest in ways that raise productivity.

According to demographer Andrew Mason, this secondary impact on productivity was an important driver of the economic miracle in East and Southeast Asia.[5] During South Korea's postwar boom, its GDP growth rates rose or fell closely in line with changes in the dependency ratio. China's GDP growth peaked in 2010, the same year the dependency ratio bottomed out at one dependent for every three workers and started to climb.

The best-positioned countries are those taking steps to keep older people working and out of the "dependent" population. While retirees weigh on growth, an older labor force with a high share of experienced workers tends to be more productive. In 2007, Germany increased the retirement age from 65 to 67 for both men and women, to be phased in gradually. European countries including Italy and Portugal have pegged changes in the retirement age to increases in life expectancy, and others are debating a retirement age of 70 or more. There are holdouts, but pushing back the retirement age is a positive sign for aging economies, adding both workers and output per worker.

What Happened to Women in the Workforce?

The worldwide movement of women into the workforce that energized much of the postwar era has stagnated in the past twenty years, with the average female labor force participation rate stuck at around 50 percent.

To get a sense of which economies have the most to gain from tapping female labor, compare countries in the same income class. Among rich countries, according to Organisation for Co-operation and Development (OECD) figures for 2019, female labor force participation ranges from 80 percent in Switzerland to 73 percent in Japan and just 68 percent in the United States.

But government moves can change these numbers quickly. In 1990, only 68 percent of Canadian women participated in the workforce, but that figure has since risen to 76 percent, owing to tax cuts for second earners and new childcare services. In Japan, Prime Minister Abe has incorporated "womenomics" into his plan to revive the economy, and female labor force participation has risen from 65 to 72 percent during his five years in office. In the Netherlands, the share of women active in the workforce has doubled since 1980, to 76 percent today, as a result of expanded parental leave policies and flexible working hours. In short order, the Netherlands raced past the United States in terms of utilizing the talents of its women.

The countries with the most to gain are those with the worst gender imbalances. The OECD has estimated that if its member nations could eliminate the gender gap by the year 2030—bringing as large a share of adult women into the workforce as men—the GDP gains would peak at close to 20 percent in Japan and South

Korea and more than 20 percent in Italy, where less than 40 percent of women are in the formal labor force.

Scrapping outdated laws can provide a quick boost. In a 2014 survey of 143 emerging countries, the World Bank found that 90 percent have at least one law that limits opportunities for women. Russia still has Soviet-era laws that rope off over 450 occupations as "too strenuous for women." Other nations ban women from owning property, opening a bank account, signing a contract, entering a courtroom, traveling alone, driving, or controlling family finances.[6] Such restrictions are particularly prevalent in the Middle East and South Asia, the regions with the lowest female labor force participation rates: 26 and 35 percent, respectively.

The barriers to removing these laws are surmountable. Latin America, despite its macho reputation, is making gains. Between 1990 and 2013, five countries increased female labor force participation by more than 10 percentage points, and they were all Latin. In first place was Colombia, where the share of women active in the workforce rose by 26 percentage points, followed by Peru, Chile, Brazil, and Mexico. In a country like Brazil, where fewer men are working, the economy would have slowed a lot more if women were not stepping in to fill their places.[7] To get a bigger economic boost from working women, many countries can start by just lifting existing restrictions.

Welcome, Robot

The last pool of available talent is bottomless but controversial: robots. Today, many writers warn that the automation revolution threatens to render human labor obsolete. Unlike nineteenth-century technologies such as the loom, they argue, the latest advances are not machines designed for one task, but automatons with artificial intelligence that are capable of "machine learning" and will rapidly replace humans even in thinking professions, such as law and medicine.

This logic echoes arguments we have heard before. According to Berkeley's Machine Intelligence Research Institute, the standard forecast for when artificial intelligence will "arrive" is the same today as it was in 1955: in five years.

The automation revolution is still likely to be gradual enough to complement rather than destroy the human workforce. The world's industrial robot population of about 2.1 million is growing, but it is still dwarfed by the 247 million humans in the global industrial labor force. Most industrial robots are still unintelligent machines, committed to a single task, like turning a bolt, and nearly half are in the car industry, which is still the single largest employer (of humans) in the United States.

Workplaces evolve to incorporate machines, and people find a way to fit in. Addressing fears of a jobless future, the Harvard economist Lawrence Katz has remarked, "We never run out of jobs. There is no long-term trend of eliminating work for people."[8] Though US banks have installed many thousands of automated tellers, the savings have allowed them to open up a lot more branches, so that in total, the number of human tellers actually increased from 500,000 in 1980 to 550,000 in 2010.

If automation were displacing humans as fast as is implied in recent books like Martin Ford's *The Rise of the Robots*, then we would be seeing a negative impact on jobs. We're not. After the crisis of 2008, economic growth was weak, but job growth was unusually strong in major industrial countries, compared to earlier recoveries. In fact the job picture has been particularly strong in Germany, Japan, and South Korea, the industrial countries that employ the most robots.

The practical answer to fewer young workers is, arguably, more robots. An interviewer recently asked the Nobel economist Daniel Kahneman about the threat that robots pose to employment in China. "You just don't get it," Kahneman responded. "In China, the robots are going to come just in time" to rescue the economy from population decline.[9] Beijing does get it, and now subsidizes industrial automation.

Over the past quarter century, as the consulting firm McKinsey & Company has pointed out, about a third of the new jobs created in the United States were types that did not exist, or barely existed, twenty-five years ago. In the next transformation, humans are likely to replace jobs lost to automation with new jobs we can't yet imagine. And economists may start counting growth in the robot population as a positive sign for economic growth, the same way that today they analyze growth in the human population.

To assess whether population trends are pushing a nation to rise or to fall, look first at growth in the working-age population, which sets a baseline for how fast the economy can grow. Then track what countries are doing to bring more workers into the talent pool, quickly. Are they opening doors to the elderly, to women, to foreigners, even to robots? In a world facing the challenge of growing labor shortages, it's all hands—human or automated—on deck.

2

POLITICS

Successful Nations Rally behind a Reformer

I n the circle of political life, crisis forces a nation to reform, reform leads to good times, and good times encourage an arrogance that leads to a new crisis.

I have seen this pattern over and over. Even a figure like Vladimir Putin, now widely castigated as a dictator, came to power as a reformer out of necessity, following the financial crises that battered Russia in the 1990s. He kept his head down, pushed economic discipline, simplified a byzantine tax system, and began saving oil profits. Over the next decade, his nation's average income quintupled, to around $12,000, encouraging complacency among ordinary Russians and arrogance in the Kremlin. Intoxicated by sky-high approval ratings, Putin quit pushing reform and began tightening his hold on power. In 2014, a new crisis hit as oil prices collapsed. Russia's average per capita income fell by nearly a third, to $8,000, and five years later it has yet to fully recover.

These relapses are commonplace. In the emerging world, growth is much less steady than in the developed world, and it is marked by sharper upturns and more prolonged downturns. Often the downturns are painful enough to wipe out gains made during the booms, limiting a nation's progress over time. While politics can shape the economy of developed nations, it matters even more in emerging countries, where institutions tend to be weaker, and one man or woman at the top can make all the difference.

Successful nations throw their political weight behind a reformer, frequently one new to office. Often they are most likely to change for the better when they are in the early stage of the circle of life: in the depths of crisis, ready to back a serious reformer. On the far end of the circle, they are most likely to change for the worse in boom times, when the populace is sinking into complacency, accepting an aging leader, forgetting that in a competitive world the need to reform is constant.

The most auspicious moment is the arrival of the right leader, at the right time. Putin fit this profile when he assumed power in 1999 and immediately launched sweeping reforms.

The least auspicious periods come during good times, when even reformers tend to grow stale and overconfident, and begin hanging on to power by extending government largesse to powerful allies and to a complacent populace. By 2008, Putin fit this profile too. Many others have followed the same trajectory, from agent of change to obstacle to further reform, including Suharto of Indonesia, Mahathir Mohamad in Malaysia, and Recep Tayyip Erdoğan in Turkey.

I have a couple of guidelines for spotting the leaders most likely to shape popular support for reform into a workable program, at least for the next five years. The probability of successful reform is higher under fresh leaders than stale leaders, under leaders with a mass base than well-credentialed technocrats, and under democratic leaders than autocrats.

Fresh Leaders

The bigger the crisis, the more eagerly people will support a powerful leader capable of disrupting the old order. Or as French president Charles de Gaulle once put it, "History is the encounter of will and exceptional periods."[1]

The first big shock to postwar prosperity came in the 1970s, as economic growth stagnated and inflation took off on the back of runaway welfare-state spending and oil price shocks. As in any crisis, some nations turned to populists promising easy answers and national glory, but by the 1980s, a few had turned to pioneering reformers, led by Margaret Thatcher in Britain, Ronald Reagan in the United States, and Deng Xiaoping in China.

In these cases, the precipitating crisis was less a sudden shock than a slow-burning fear of losing economic stature. Thatcher and Reagan both vowed to turn back "socialism" and to make up for the humiliations of the 1970s, when Britain became the first developed nation to seek an IMF bailout and the United States was humbled by the OPEC oil price hikes. Deng, in turn, had visited Singapore and New York and had seen that these capitalist economies were far ahead of his own.

The stagflation of the 1970s was traceable in varying degrees to cumbersome state controls, and the solution pushed by this generation of leaders created a basic template for cutting back the state. In the United States and Britain, reform included some mix of loosening central control over the economy, cutting taxes and red tape, privatizing state companies, and lifting price controls. In China, it included freeing peasants to till their own land and opening to foreign trade and investment. As the United States and Britain started to recover in the 1980s, and particularly as China's economy took off, these role models helped to inspire other reformers.

By the 1990s, under the new free market orthodoxy, many emerging nations started to open up to outside trade and capital flows, and some started borrowing heavily from foreign creditors. Induced by these rising debts, currency crises struck in Mexico in 1994, spread through Asia in 1997–98, and then leapfrogged to Russia, Turkey, and Brazil. The circle of life was turning, as these crises generated popular support for a new generation of leaders: Kim Dae-jung in South Korea, Luiz Inácio Lula da Silva in Brazil, Erdoğan in Turkey, and Putin in Russia.

This quartet brought runaway spending under control, laying the foundation of budget and trade surpluses, shrinking debts, and falling inflation that helped to underpin the greatest boom ever to lift the developing world. In the five years before 2010, 107 of 110 emerging nations for which there is data saw their per capita income rise relative to that of the United States. That catch-up rate of 97 percent compares to an average of 42 percent for every previous five-year period going back fifty years. All the reasonably large emerging economies were catching up, and the leaders of South Korea, Russia, Turkey, and Brazil contributed more than any other leaders to what became known as "the rise of the rest."[2]

Kim Dae-jung of South Korea was arguably the most impressive change agent in this group. A charismatic dissident who had been jailed repeatedly by authoritarian regimes of the 1970s and '80s, he finally won election at the height of the Asian financial crisis in 1998. He set about breaking up the secretive ties among politicians, state banks, and leading conglomerates that had allowed Korean companies to run up the massive debts that melted down in the crisis. No member of this leadership generation did more to reform the basic structure of his nation's economy, which is one reason South Korea remains economically stronger than Russia, Turkey, or Brazil.

Still, the accomplishments of Kim's peers were also remarkable. Taking the advice of reformers like Russian finance minister Alexei Kudrin, Putin attacked the corruption inherent in a byzantine tax system by cutting the number of taxes from 200 to 16, combining multiple income tax rates into a low flat rate, replacing multiple collection agencies with one, and even firing all the tax police. The reforms raised revenue and helped stabilize the national finances for the first time since the collapse of the Soviet Union.

In 2003, Erdoğan took office in Turkey, and he, too, listened to clearheaded advice about how to fix his nation's finances. He reformed a wasteful pension system, privatized state banks, passed a law to shut down bankrupt companies more smoothly, and vowed to maintain a budget surplus. Over the next decade, the Turks, like the Russians, would see their average per capita income rise many times over, to more than $10,000. Both countries would move from the ranks of poor nations to the middle class, at least for a while.

One natural objection to this argument is that Russia and Turkey were growing in the midst of a global boom, no credit to Putin or Erdoğan. While good luck and global circumstances were part of the story, good policies helped boost Russia and Turkey, which enjoyed more solid growth and lower inflation during this period than did economies under less responsible populists, like Hugo Chávez in Venezuela and Néstor Kirchner in Argentina.

The same mix of good luck and good policy marked the rise of Lula in Brazil. Elected in 2002, he replaced Fernando Henrique Cardoso, a reformer who had started the fight against hyperinflation. But it was the left-wing radical Lula who had the charisma and street credibility to finish the job. He installed an inflation fighter in the central bank, setting the stage for a steady boom. Following in the footsteps of strong economic leaders before him, Lula combined a basic understanding of what his country needed to recover with the popular touch needed to sell hard reform, and thus he helped to extricate his country from an exceptionally difficult period.

Stale Leaders

One simple way to think about this rule is that high-impact reform is most likely in a leader's first term, and less likely in the second term and beyond, as a leader runs out of ideas or support for reform and turns to securing a grand legacy, or riches for friends and family. There are exceptions—Lee Kuan Yew governed Singapore for more than three decades and never seemed to lose energy for reform—but the general pattern holds. In the end, said the American essayist Ralph Waldo Emerson, every hero becomes a bore.

Even Reagan fell victim to the "second-term curse," that cycle of scandal, popular fatigue, and congressional opposition that has made it tough for American presidents to push change after their first terms. Thatcher never lost her zeal for reform, but even fellow conservatives tired of her uncompromising style and pushed her out after twelve years. Deng, arguably the most important economic reformer of the twentieth century, had ruled for only nine years when he lost his titles as military and party chief following the 1989 uprising at Tiananmen Square. That episode sets a striking benchmark for the political life span of even the best economic leaders. By then, China had imposed a two-term limit to prevent leaders from hanging on too long, but it effectively lifted that ban in 2018 for Xi Jinping, making him president for as long as he wishes.

Today, both Erdoğan and Putin are in their fourth terms in top posts, and they are particularly ripe examples of stale leadership. By the time his third term began in 2011, Erdoğan was abandoning economic reform, enforcing Islamic social mores more aggressively, and spending lavishly to re-create what he saw as the Islamic greatness that had been Turkey in the Ottoman era. In 2013, Erdoğan's plan to turn a popular Istanbul park into an Ottoman-inspired mall would envelop Turkey in a broad middle-class revolt against aging governments across the emerging world.

Writers racing to explain these revolts focused on the rise of the middle class, and its demands for political freedom, but there was a problem with this analysis. Over the previous fifteen years, in twenty-one of the largest emerging nations, the middle class had expanded by an average of 18 percentage points as a share of the total population, to a bit more than half.[3] The protests, however, had erupted in nations where the middle class had grown very fast, such as Russia, or quite slowly, such as South Africa. The biggest protests hit countries where the middle class was expanding at a pace close to the 18-point average: Egypt, Brazil, and Turkey. In short, there was no clear link between growth in the middle class and the location or intensity of the protests.

However, every one of these protests targeted an aging regime. Though just about every emerging economy was lifted up by the global boom of the early twenty-first century, many leaders took personal credit for this success and started playing tricks—dodging term limits, switching from the prime minister's office to the presidency—to hang on to power. Between 2003 and 2013, among the twenty most important emerging economies, the average tenure of the ruling party doubled from four years to eight years.

By 2013, seven of the twenty most important emerging economies were suffering political unrest: Russia, India, South Africa, Egypt, Turkey, Brazil, and Argentina. And every one of those outbreaks targeted a regime that had been in power more than eight years; this was a revolt against stale leaders.

The stock markets sense this decay. Since 1988, the major emerging countries have held more than 100 national elections, producing seventy-six new leaders. Nineteen of those leaders, including Putin, Erdoğan, Lula, and Manmohan Singh of India, lasted two full terms in office. As their tenures wore on, the stock markets turned on the entire group. These markets outperformed the global average for emerging markets by 16 percent in the leader's first term, then barely matched the global average in the second term.

To pinpoint the moment when markets tend to turn on seated

leaders, I looked at the same set of elections and identified leaders who lasted at least five years. For this group of thirty-nine leaders, the stock market outperformed the emerging-world average by close to 20 percent in the first 43 months of the leaders' tenure—with close to 80 percent of that gain coming in just the first 24 months. After 43 months, the market started to move sideways. This finding looks like strong confirmation that emerging-world leaders are most likely to push significant economic reform in their early years; markets, of course, tend to go up when investors have reason to expect the economy to accelerate and inflation to decline.

The same analysis for developed countries revealed no clear connection between stock market returns and aging regimes. This lack of a link doesn't suggest that leaders don't matter in developed economies—only that they can produce much bigger growth swings in developing economies. Sensing that, markets respond more sharply to politics in the emerging world.

Populist Demagogues versus Populists Who Get It

Successful leaders often share two key attributes: support among the masses, and a clear understanding of economic reform, or at least a willingness to delegate policy to experts. In contrast, demagogues who artfully combine populism and nationalism can be politically successful but tend to be a disaster for the economy.

Consider the way Venezuela and neighboring Colombia parted ways following the crises of the 1990s. In 2002, Venezuelans elected radical populist Hugo Chávez, who pushed an experimental socialism under which Venezuelan incomes have continued a half century of decline. The same year, Colombia elected right-wing populist Álvaro Uribe, who put the books in order and managed to quell the guerrilla uprisings that had upended the economy for decades. Uribe was hugely popular; in his first term the Colombian stock market rose more than 1,600 percent—the biggest increase for any of the sixty-three first-term leaders in my study.

The best leaders often combine public charisma and private earnestness. Deng Xiaoping was a visionary reformer and magnetic public personality, yet in private he could surprise visitors like Henry Kissinger with detailed updates on such subjects as the accomplishments of the department of metallurgy. Benigno "Noynoy" Aquino, the Philippine president from 2010 to 2016, was not in the same league as a reformer but had similar qualities. Aquino could speak at length on subjects like local sardine fisheries—exactly the kind of brass-tacks reformer the Philippines needed after a string of flamboyantly corrupt leaders.

The global markets often make no distinction between reckless and practical populists, or they project their own hopes for business-friendly reform onto an election. In 2014 the markets were stunned by the victory of the left-wing candidate Dilma Rousseff in Brazil, in part because market analysts lost sight of how often nations facing economic trouble will respond to a mix of nationalism and populism. By early 2019, markets were hopeful about the rise of business-friendly conservative governments across Latin America, only to see those new regimes stumble in the face of popular protests in Brazil, Argentina, Chile, and Peru.

The False Dawn of the Technocrats

The markets tend to cheer for technocrats, assuming that leaders with backgrounds at the World Bank or a prestigious university will understand the requirements of strong growth. But technocrats rarely succeed in national leadership roles, because they often lack the flair to sell reform. The European Commission president Jean-Claude Juncker captured the lament of technocrats everywhere when he remarked, "We all know what to do, we just don't know how to get re-elected after we've done it."[4]

During the euro crisis of 2010, several nations turned to technocratic leaders. Greece brought in former central bank chief Lucas Papademos; the Czech Republic appointed former national chief statistician Jan Fischer. Italy put its hopes in Mario Monti, a former university president and European commissioner. None lasted much more than a year. In 2011, Italy's stock market rose on reports that Monti would be prime minister, but typically, he made necessary austerity moves and failed to sell them to the public. He lost the next election, taking just 10 percent of the vote.

Authoritarian states have been perhaps the most avid believers in technocratic expertise. The Soviet Union collapsed in part because of its devotion to pseudoscientific central planning, and its obsession influenced many other countries, including dictatorships like East Germany and democracies like India under the Congress Party or Mexico during the seventy-one-year rule of the Institutional Revolutionary Party (PRI).

On the other hand, technocrats can serve reformers well, if they are giving the right advice and leaders are willing to listen.

Former World Bank economist Vikram Nehru tells a story about the bank's point man in Asia, Bernard Bell, during the 1960s. Bell advised countries with a menu of ideas on how to boost exports and open to global trade, but not every nation was ready to hear him. In India he was greeted with a headline saying, in effect, "Bernie Bell Go to Hell." Then he went to Indonesia, where President Suharto was so impressed that he asked the bank to appoint Bell as its representative in Jakarta. Bell served there from 1968 to 1972, and with a circle of advisers known as the "Berkeley Mafia" he helped to put Indonesia on track to become a mini–Asian miracle over the next two decades.

This model can be effective: technocrats serving an autocratic regime, which can implement ideas rapidly. The trouble comes when those in power ignore popular sentiment. In 1990s Argentina, President Carlos Menem appointed his own team of US-trained experts, who experimented with currency controls that stabilized the peso but eventually led to mounting debt and an outright depression, which began in 1998. The economy contracted by nearly 30 percent over the next four years, leaving behind a populace that to this day is deeply suspicious of technocrats bearing big ideas for reform.

China is the very different case of a successful technocracy that may be growing too confident. For years, China reported much less volatile economic growth than other developing nations, creating suspicion that it was manipulating the numbers. I thought that suspicion was overblown; Deng Xiaoping's underlings did not always report that growth was hitting the target.

The situation changed in 2012, when authorities began reporting that growth was coming within a few decimal points of its official target, and they continue to claim this uncanny accuracy seven years later. At one point a top Chinese official went so far as to declare that the leadership would not "tolerate" growth below 7 percent, as if they could forbid slowdowns in an $8 trillion economy. Throughout, China has based its target on calculations of how fast the economy needs to grow to catch the United States—a political target reminiscent of those that guided the Soviet Union's effort to bury the West. We all know how that attempt ended. It is not possible to engineer endless runs of fast growth, and that lesson applies to all technocrats, even the successful ones in Beijing.

Bullets versus Ballots

The long boom in China, which dates back to the late 1970s, led many people to believe that autocracies are better than democracies at generating long runs of growth, and it's true that autocrats do have some distinct advantages. They can ignore or overrun opposition, and that freedom allows the few visionaries among them to accomplish a lot more than democratic rivals do. Autocratic leaders have presided over enduring economic miracles in South Korea under Park Chung-hee, and in Taiwan under Chiang Kai-shek and his son. But these are exceptional cases.

Over the last three decades, there were 124 cases in which a nation posted GDP growth faster than 5 percent for a full decade, and 64 of those growth spells came under the rule of a democratic regime, 60 under an authoritarian regime. In general, autocrats are no more likely to produce long runs of strong growth.

Authoritarian systems also have glaring economic weaknesses. Because the top leader faces no opposition at the ballot box, the threat of regimes growing stale looms large. As the New York University development expert William Easterly has pointed out, for every long run of 10 percent growth produced by an autocrat like Deng Xiaoping, there were several long periods of stagnation under a Castro in Cuba, a Kim in North Korea, or a Mugabe in Zimbabwe.[5] Once an authoritarian regime is forced to hold elections, it loses its power to force rapid growth, but as a democracy it gains an incentive to let growth rise naturally by, for example, respecting property rights and breaking up state monopolies.

Because of their unchecked power, autocrats are also much more likely to produce destabilizing swings between high and low growth. Looking at records going back to 1950 for 150 countries, I found 43 cases in which the economy grew at an average annual rate of 7 percent or more for a full decade. The majority of these booms—35—unfolded under an authoritarian government. These cases include the Asian "miracle economies" that kept growth alive for several decades. But they also include many economies that stumbled after one strong decade, including Venezuela, which stalled in the 1960s, Iran in the 1970s, and Syria in the 1980s.

Long slumps are also much more common under authoritarian rule. Since 1950, there have been 138 cases in which, over the course of a full decade, a nation posted an average annual growth rate of less than 3 percent—which feels like a recession in emerging countries. And 100 of those cases unfolded under authoritarian regimes, ranging from Ghana in the 1950s and '60s to Saudi Arabia and Romania in the 1980s, and Nigeria in the 1990s. The

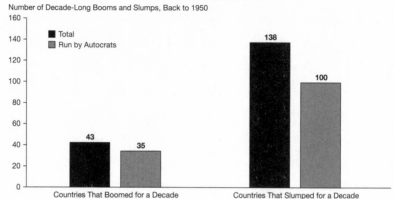

Extreme Growth in Autocracies

Number of Decade-Long Booms and Slumps, Back to 1950

Source: World Bank, Haver Analytics, Politi-Score.

critical flaw of autocracies is this tendency toward extreme, volatile outcomes.

In the worst cases—economies that toggle between rapid growth and recession—the government is usually authoritarian. Looking back to 1950, there are 36 countries that have seen frequent extreme swings, with years of growth above 7 percent alternating with years of negative growth. Whipsawed in this way, it is impossible for people to lead a normal life. And 27 of these traumatized countries—including Iran, Ethiopia, Iraq, Syria, and Nigeria—were governed by an authoritarian regime for most of this period. Most of these countries are very poor to this day, with average incomes below $5,000, because the boom years were wiped out by bust years.

Sometimes these extreme booms and busts unfold under a single dictator, who refuses to leave, despite the chaos he creates. The most dizzying dictator was Saddam Hussein, who ran Iraq for twenty-five years, through 2003, with more than three-fourths of those years marked by extreme high or low growth. Close behind is Hafez al-Assad, who ran Syria for thirty years, until 2000; nearly two-thirds of those years were marked by extreme growth.

In contrast, democracies dominate the list of countries with the steadiest growth. Together, Sweden, France, Belgium, and Norway have posted only one year of growth faster than 7 percent since 1950. But over that time, these four democracies have all seen their average incomes increase five- to sixfold, to a minimum of more than $30,000, in part because they rarely suffered full years of negative growth.

This is the stabilizing effect of democracy, and it accounts for a simple fact: every large economy that has seen average income grow to more than $10,000 is a democracy. China, with an average income approaching $10,000, is trying to become a large, rich autocracy, but it would be the first. Anyone looking for nations that can grow steadily into the wealthy class should not bet on autocrats.

The Circle of Life

The fact that crisis and revolt can force elites to reform has been clear at least since the early critiques of Marx, who thought capitalism would collapse in a series of increasingly violent attempts to defend the upper classes. Instead, leaders proved capable of reforming capitalism, deflecting popular revolt by creating the welfare state, starting in Germany and Britain.

The link between boom times and political complacency is equally well documented—for example, in the cases of modern Japan and Europe, which are often described as too comfortably rich to push tough reform. What is less well recognized is that even in normal periods, the circle of life turns, constantly reshaping economies for better or worse.

The circle turns erratically, even in democracies where elections are regularly scheduled. Nations may wallow in complacency for years, which helps explain why the "lost decades" in Africa and Latin America lasted longer than a decade. On the other hand, strong-willed leaders have been known to keep pushing reform for decades—but only in the rare "miracle" cases, including Korea, Taiwan, and Japan before it fell off the miracle path in 1990.

Modern economies thus follow a cycle similar to that of energy and matter—exploding in crisis, only to re-form and revive before dying out once again. The circle of life tells you that the likely timing and direction of change depends in part on where a country stands on the cycle of crisis, reform, boom, and decay. In general, the fortunes of a nation are most likely to turn for the better when a new leader rises in the wake of a crisis, and most likely to decline when a stale leader is in power.

The circle of life also helps explain why so few booms last long enough to vault developing economies into the developed ranks, and why those that make the leap are called "miracles": they have defied the natural complacency and decay that kills most long booms.

3

INEQUALITY

Successful Nations Produce Good Billionaires

Until recently, wealth inequality was often downplayed as a social issue, too soft to shape an economic forecast, despite the growing body of research showing that rising inequality can undermine growth in at least three ways: by discouraging mass consumption, rewarding corruption, and fueling political resentment against wealth creation.

Rich people tend to save more, if only because there is a limit to how much more they can spend on material goods like food, clothing, appliances, and cars. So, when more of the national income goes to the rich, they spend less of this additional income than the poor or middle class would, and the economy slows. The way economists put it is that the rich have a lower "marginal propensity to consume."

Wealth inequality also both reflects and encourages capital misallocation, as entrenched political elites steer government business and protection to favored cronies, diverting funds away from the most efficient businesses and the most productive investment targets.[1]

The spectacle of wealth concentrating in the hands of a narrow elite can also provoke revolts against the whole idea of wealth creation. In the postwar period, for example, Latin America has enjoyed spells of rapid growth as frequently as Asia has, but Latin growth spells are more likely to be short and to end in "hard landings." Why? IMF researchers Andrew Berg and Jonathan Ostry argue that the strongest explanation is the colonial-era legacy of rampant inequality in Latin America, which "may impede growth at least in part *because* it calls forth efforts to redistribute that themselves undercut growth."[2]

In many cases these efforts appear as more or less heavy-handed attempts to spread the wealth through higher taxes or regulation or welfare spending, as was the case in many developed nations by 2019.

All too often, the backlash brings to power a populist firebrand who delivers radical redistribution in a way that burns down the economy. In extreme cases, these demagogues seize private businesses, ban foreign investors, raise taxes to choking levels in the name of helping the poor, and rapidly expand the government and spending on wasteful subsidies.

This growth-killing agenda has been pursued by populists in every region of the world, from Robert Mugabe of Zimbabwe to Kim Il-sung of North Korea and Zulfikar Ali Bhutto of Pakistan. But their epicenter is Latin America, where the list of populists pushing radical redistribution extends from Fidel Castro of Cuba in the 1950s through Juan Velasco Alvarado of Peru in the late 1960s, Luis Echeverría Álvarez of Mexico in the 1970s, Daniel Ortega of

Nicaragua in the 1980s, Hugo Chávez of Venezuela in the 1990s, and Néstor Kirchner of Argentina in the early years of the twenty-first century.

The economic impact of inequality is likely to grow because inequality has been rising worldwide, particularly for measures of wealth, for decades. It began to widen even faster after central banks, responding to the global financial crisis of 2008, began to loosen monetary policy aggressively. Though intended to fuel investment in new plants and business ventures, much of this easy money was diverted into purchases of stocks, luxury homes, and other financial assets, pushing up prices. Since the wealthiest people own the bulk of these assets, they got richer the fastest.

The poor were not getting poorer, but the wealth of the rich, and particularly the superrich, was growing faster. Between 2009 and 2019, despite the weak global economy, the number of billionaires worldwide more than doubled, from 1,011 to 2,153, and their combined fortunes rose from $3.6 trillion to $8.7 trillion. The boom helped bring to power anti-elite populists on the left and right, including, ironically, a self-proclaimed champion of the blue-collar working class who also claimed to be a billionaire, President Donald Trump.

The challenge is how to track inequality—and the threat it poses to economic growth—in real time. The most common measure of income inequality, the Gini coefficient, is derived from official data by academics, using a variety of methods, published on no particular schedule and for no consistent sample of countries. Often, the most recent Gini score for any given country can be five to ten years out of date.

My approach uses a forensic reading of the *Forbes* billionaire list, which is at least updated annually and has evolved so that it tracks shifts in billionaire wealth daily. To identify nations in which tycoons are taking a large and growing share of the pie, I calculate the scale of billionaire wealth relative to the size of the economy. To identify countries in which tycoons are becoming an entrenched elite, I estimate the share of inherited wealth in the billionaire ranks.

Billionaire Index: Emerging Countries

Country	Total Billionaire Wealth/GDP	Bad Billionaires' Wealth/Total Billionaire Wealth	Inherited Billionaires' Wealth/ Total Billionaire Wealth
Brazil	9%	3%	38%
China	7%	30%	3%
India	14%	29%	60%
Indonesia	7%	8%	68%
Mexico	11%	67%	42%
Poland	2%	0%	27%
Russia	26%	69%	0%
South Korea	6%	6%	59%
Taiwan	14%	9%	38%
Turkey	6%	17%	40%
Emerging-Country Average	10%	24%	37%

Source: Data from *Forbes* billionaires list.

Billionaire Index: Developed Countries

Country	Total Billionaire Wealth/GDP	Bad Billionaires' Wealth/Total Billionaire Wealth	Inherited Billionaires' Wealth/ Total Billionaire Wealth
Australia	8%	50%	33%
Canada	9%	17%	43%
France	12%	8%	78%
Germany	13%	13%	70%
Italy	7%	7%	55%
Japan	2%	14%	15%
Sweden	23%	13%	73%
Switzerland	15%	13%	50%
United Kingdom	6%	22%	16%
United States	15%	14%	30%
Developed-Country Average	11%	17%	46%

Source: Data from *Forbes* billionaires list.

Most important, I track the wealth of "bad billionaires" in industries long associated with corruption, such as oil or mining or real estate. It is the rise of an entrenched class of bad billionaires in traditionally corruption-prone and unproductive industries that is most likely to choke off growth and to feed the popular anger on which populist demagogues thrive. Successful nations generate good billionaires, or at least more good ones than bad ones.

Scale: Shockingly Large Billionaire Shares of the Wealth

The advantage of screening three ways is that it will identify nations where the billionaire class is vulnerable to political attack for its scale, family ties, or political connections. Any one of those avenues can generate popular resentment.

I started building this system around 2010, amid growing outrage in India over news media exposés about how a corrupt elite had wormed its way to the top in parliament, industry, even Bollywood movies. To check the popular story line, I scanned the billionaire list for that year and found that the top ten Indian tycoons controlled wealth equal to a stunning 12 percent of GDP—compared to only 1 percent in China. The perception that India suffered from an unusual concentration of wealth seemed to have some truth to it, but when I pressed high officials on this point, they dismissed inequality and corruption as normal conditions in a developing country. Early-twentieth-century America had its robber barons too, they argued. Many of these officials would change their tune, however, as the Indian growth rate slowed by almost half in subsequent years and it became clear that corruption and inequality were key factors in the slowdown.

Crony capitalism steers money and deals to undeserving hands and sets off a chain reaction in the political system. India's courts began in 2010 to punish high-profile businessmen, holding them in jail for months before filing charges, pressuring the Central Bureau of Investigation to pursue cases aggressively, even if evidence was thin. Bureaucrats feared granting business anything, even routine permits. In 2015, Indian finance minister Arun Jaitley said that investigative "overkill" had "hindered the whole process of economic decision-making."[3] At this point it was hard to tell which was worse for the economy—crony capitalism and inequality, or the battle to root it out. India had lost its balance.

One way to tell whether billionaire wealth threatens to destabilize a country is to compare it with its peers. In the 2010s, total billionaire wealth has averaged about 10 percent of GDP, in both developed and large emerging economies, and any share above 15 percent is a significant outlier. Among emerging nations, Russia has suffered extreme wealth inequality since it began selling off state companies after the fall of Communism. The corrupt privatization process created a new class of oligarchs in the 1990s and turned Moscow into an open-air showroom for Bugatti and Bentley. Today, Russia has close to 100 billionaires, far more than many much larger economies, and they control fortunes equal to an astonishing 26 percent of GDP, the largest share of any country in my index.

No other emerging country is so top-heavy with wealth. Though Chile and Malaysia have in recent years also seen billionaire wealth swell dangerously, as of 2019 the only emerging economies where the billionaire share of GDP approached 15 percent were India and, surprisingly, Taiwan. Though Taiwan was one of the few nations that managed to produce a long postwar run of high growth with no spike in inequality, today Taiwan billionaires control wealth equal to 14 percent of GDP, up from 9 percent a decade earlier. The fact that most of them are in tech and other relatively uncorrupt industries, and that the inherited share of their wealth is (at 37 percent) pretty typical for an emerging country, helps explain why the scale of their fortunes has so far not become a hot political issue.

Billionaire elites also control bloated fortunes in some developed nations—none more unexpected than Sweden. Despite its egalitarian image, Sweden turned to the right after a financial crisis in the early 1990s, cutting taxes and welfare payments. Since then, Sweden's economy has grown more steadily than most of its peers, but so has inequality. Sweden has only thirty-three billionaires, but that number is up by ten in recent years, and their wealth is now equal to 23 percent of GDP, up from 17 percent in 2010. That proportion would be extreme even by emerging-world standards, and it helps explain how the Social Democrats staged a comeback in 2014, promising to raise taxes on the rich, and still hung on to power—though just barely—five years later.

Despite its reputation for winner-take-all capitalism, the United States until this decade had a medium-sized billionaire class, with fortunes equal to roughly 10 percent of GDP—close to the global average. That share increased to 15 percent by 2014, where it remains today, driven in part by easy money pouring out of the Federal Reserve, and by the rise of Silicon Valley tycoons.

On the flip side, it is normally a healthy sign when billionaire wealth is below the global average of 10 percent of GDP. It seems fair to say, for example, that in countries where billionaire wealth is around 5 percent of GDP or less, such as Poland or South Korea, the scale of the billionaires' fortunes is not large enough to become a target for serious social unrest.

The exception to that rule is a country like Japan, where relatively small billionaire fortunes may reflect a chronic incapacity to create wealth. Some academic research shows that growth tends to slow not only when inequality is very high but also when it is very low.[4] Japan's billionaire class may be too small for the nation's good, and some Japanese seem to realize this. They have a word, *akubyodo*, which translates as "bad egalitarianism" and describes a leveling culture that rewards seniority more than merit and risk-taking. It's not a good sign when rainmakers are seen as inherently disreputable.

Quality: The Good versus Bad Billionaires

Looking at the scale of billionaire fortunes is not enough to reveal the extent of their political vulnerabilities. New names on the billionaire list can be a favorable sign, but only if they are good billionaires, emerging outside "rent-seeking industries" such as construction, real estate, gambling, mining, steel, aluminum, oil, gas, and other commodity sectors that mainly involve digging resources out of the ground. In these businesses, major players often spend their time extracting maximum rents from limited national resources by bribing politicians if necessary, not growing national wealth in innovative ways.

To make a qualitative judgment about the sources of great fortunes, I compare the total wealth of tycoons in these corruption-prone businesses to that of all billionaires in the country. This comparison yields the share of the wealth generated by "bad billionaires." This label no doubt miscasts many honest mining and oil tycoons, but even in nations where these industries are relatively uncorrupt, they tend to make weak contributions to productivity, and to tie the economy to the volatile swings of commodity prices.

My assumption is that other billionaires make a greater contribution, but I reserve the "good billionaire" label for tycoons in industries that are known to make the largest contributions to growth in productivity, or that make popular consumer products like smartphones or cars. These "good" industries are the ones least likely to generate backlashes against wealth creation; they include technology, manufacturing, pharmaceuticals, and telecoms, as well as retail, e-commerce, and entertainment.*

To be clear, the billionaire analysis does not generate hard data but does offer anecdotally telling, real-time evidence of how nations are generating wealth. Among the largest developed economies, as of 2019, bad billionaires controlled the smallest shares of billionaire wealth in Italy (7 percent) and France (8 percent)—a good sign for both countries.

In Sweden, the scarcity of bad billionaires has taken some edge off the backlash against their bloated share of the economy. Only 13 percent of Swedish billionaire wealth originates in rent-seeking

---

* In a few cases, I counted tycoons in good industries as bad billionaires, because of well-documented ties to political corruption.

industries. Much of the rest is created at globally competitive companies, including H&M in fashion and IKEA in furniture retailing. These companies are making the most of their revenue abroad and pulling money into Sweden—not battling to dominate domestic resources.

For years, the prevalence of good billionaires had a similar impact in the United States. Many of the top ten tycoons had been around for decades, but the companies they own—Microsoft, Berkshire Hathaway, Oracle, and Walmart—would make any economy more competitive. Figures like Warren Buffett and Bill Gates were almost folk heroes, for their business accomplishments and philanthropy, and for pressing fellow billionaires to bequeath their fortunes to charity too.

The newer generation of American tycoons, arising from tech companies like Google, Apple, and Facebook, were also emerging as pop icons, largely because consumers loved the goods and services they provide. Only in recent years did a backlash set in, as regulators and politicians began to investigate the tech giants as monopolists who profit by misusing private data and allowing hate speech to flourish online. There still is no modern equivalent to the widely despised American monopolists of the early twentieth century, when John D. Rockefeller was vilified as "public enemy number one," but figures like Facebook founder Mark Zuckerberg are starting to be viewed in this negative light. And by 2019 the backlash was generating regulatory proposals to break up or rein in their monopolies—and their capacity to generate wealth.

China's billionaire class has also been reshaped by the tech boom. The fortunes of its richest individuals surpassed $10 billion for the first time in 2014, led by internet magnates including Jack Ma of Alibaba. These decabillionaires are rising in the most liberalized and competitive private-sector businesses, not older state-dominated sectors. In recent years, however, the bad-billionaire share has climbed upward to 30 percent, close to the average for emerging nations, as real estate tycoons in particular have climbed toward the top of the list. And even some of the tech billionaires were taking seats in the National People's Congress, which is widely dismissed as a rubber-stamp legislature but does provide direct access to the top corridors of political power.

Few new or good billionaires are to be found in nations like Turkey or Russia, where aging regimes have turned away from reform and promoted favored tycoons. Eight out of every ten Turkish billionaires live in Istanbul, long the commercial center of the country, to be closer to the action. But the undisputed capital of connected tycoons is Moscow. Nearly 70 percent of Russian billionaire wealth comes from bad billionaires—one of the highest shares in the world—and seventy-one of the country's ninety-eight billionaires live in the Russian capital. These imbalances illustrate why the environment for wealth creation in Russia is so hostile. The Kremlin treats billionaires with contempt, arbitrarily changing rules that govern their businesses, knowing the public has little sympathy for a billionaire class widely perceived as corrupt.

Popular resentment against great wealth is palpable in Mexico as well, where bad billionaires also control close to 70 percent of billionaire wealth. Mexican tycoons are known for cornering industries such as telephones and concrete, which earn monopoly profits for their owners while driving up prices for consumers. The resulting anger helps explain why the Mexican rich live in fear of kidnappings for ransom, and the superrich live behind high walls and heavy security. The contrast to many developing economies in Asia and eastern Europe, where high-profile billionaires often bask in national adulation, could not be sharper.

Family Ties

Bad billionaires typically arise in family empires, particularly in the emerging world, where weaker institutions make it easier for old families to cultivate political connections. To identify nations where bloodlines are most likely to distort competition, I use *Forbes* data that distinguishes between "self-made" and "inherited" fortunes.

Among ten of the major developed economies in 2019, the inherited share of billionaire wealth was around 15 percent in Britain and Japan, slightly above 30 percent in the United States, and 70 percent or more in Germany, France, and Sweden. Sweden has been able to grow steadily over time, despite being so top-heavy with billionaires, including many who inherited their wealth, because it scores well on most of the other ten rules. Still, the fault line of rising inequality makes Sweden fertile ground for a populist backlash.

Among ten of the largest emerging economies, the range for billionaires who have inherited their wealth was even wider—from nearly 70 percent in Indonesia to 40 percent in Turkey, 3 percent in China, and 0 percent in Russia. The low share of inherited wealth in Russia and China likely owes to their relatively recent transition from Communism to market-based economic systems, which allow families to amass great wealth.

In general, heavy concentrations of family wealth are a bad sign, but the sources of family wealth matter. The low levels of inherited wealth in countries like Britain and the United States appear to reflect strong competitive environments in which new businesses can displace old ones. Even some of the oldest and most familiar names on the US billionaire list, like Gates and Zuckerberg, did not inherit wealth. They are self-made entrepreneurs. Zuckerberg is in his early thirties. By the standards of many countries, they are fresh faces.

Elsewhere, new billionaires are often not that fresh, having seen their wealth build within family companies for years, even generations. But blood ties are not always the enemy of clean and open corporate governance, particularly where the family has stepped back to play an ownership role in a publicly traded company, leaving management in professional hands. This is the model in Germany, where 70 percent of billionaire wealth is inherited but billionaire families control some of the world's most productive companies, including many of the *Mittelstand* (small to medium-sized) companies that drive the flourishing manufactured-export sector and arouse more national pride than resentment.

In Italy and France, too, there are many new names on recent billionaire lists, but most rose slowly within old family companies. Since 2010, twenty-eight new billionaires have emerged in Italy, more than half in luxury goods companies such as Prada, Dolce & Gabbana, and Bulgari. France's new billionaires also tend to rise in family firms, like Chanel and LVMH. These new billionaires are capitalizing on the competitive advantage that France and Italy have in producing fine handcrafted goods, which is part of their national identity.

For all the recent hype about a new Asia, many of its tycoons still emerge from family companies, but with only occasional stirrings of popular resentment. In South Korea, just 6 percent of billionaire wealth comes from rent-seeking industries. Many of the superrich derive their fortunes from global companies and avoid garish displays of bling. More important, while total inherited billionaire wealth remained stable in the last five years, at around $60 billion, self-made billionaire wealth nearly tripled, to more than $40 billion, driven by entrepreneurs like healthcare tycoon Seo Jung-jin and gaming magnate Kim Jung-ju. The prominence of these good billionaires has helped contain any signs of revolt against the power and influence of the wealthy in general.

The Rise of the Billionaire Rule

For much of the last decade, wealth has been rising all over the world, from the United States and Britain to China and India, mainly because of massive gains for the very rich. While in many nations all income classes are making gains, the rich are gaining faster than the poor and the middle classes. In a 2014 study of 46 major countries, Credit Suisse found that before 2007, wealth inequality was on the rise in only 12 of those countries; after 2007, that number more than doubled, to 35, from China and India to Britain and Italy.[5]

As a result, the poor are more likely to rub shoulders with the middle class, and both are more likely to live in the shadows cast by a fast-growing global billionaire class. Rising wealth inequality is an increasing threat to social stability and economic growth. It is worth tracking seriously.

Growth is particularly at risk in countries where bad billionaires are on the rise, because their success reflects deep dysfunctions: a business culture in which entrepreneurs become brazen after a run of success, a political culture in which officials grow complacent after a long period in power, an economic system in which cumbersome or nonexistent rules open the door to corrupt behavior.

Historically, political revolts against inequality have often been as destructive as the inequities themselves. Demagogues who seize private and foreign businesses in the name of redistributing wealth to the poor often end up keeping the money for themselves or their cronies—a pattern repeated with tragic frequency. Africa alone has seen this syndrome unfold under Robert Mugabe of Zimbabwe, Kenneth Kaunda of Zambia, and Julius Nyerere of Tanzania, among others.

Mugabe ruled for more than three decades, aggressively redistributing property from the old white elite to the black majority, who in many cases did not know how to farm, and appropriating vast wealth for himself and his cronies. Agricultural production collapsed, turning a food-exporting nation into an importer. When Mugabe was ousted in 2017, Zimbabwe was as poor as when he took power in 1980.

On the other hand, countries may be poised for an upturn if they are repairing the system to reduce inequality—for example, by writing land acquisition laws that fairly balance the interests of farmers and developers, as Indonesia did recently, or by holding auctions for public goods like wireless spectrum in a transparent manner that rules out backroom deals. Mexico's auction in 2015 to sell offshore oil rights drew relatively low bids, but it was a success for the system because it was conducted live on TV, which made crony deal-making unlikely.

As the number of billionaires rises, the data are becoming more significant as a statistical sample and as a tool for identifying countries where the balance of wealth is skewing too sharply to the super-rich. Tracking billionaire wealth can provide insight into whether an economy is creating the kind of wealth that will help it grow— or trigger revolt—in the near future. Tracking it by scale, share of inherited wealth, and share of bad billionaires ensures that none of these potential sources of political resentment will be missed.

It's a bad sign if the billionaire class controls too fat a share of national wealth, becomes an entrenched and inbred elite, and builds fortunes mainly from politically connected industries. A healthy economy needs an evolving cast of productive industrialists, not a fixed cast of corrupt tycoons. Creative destruction drives growth in a capitalist society, and because bad billionaires have everything to gain from the status quo, they are enemies of wider prosperity and lightning rods for populist revolts pushing to redistribute rather than grow the economic pie.

4

STATE POWER

Successful Nations Have Right-Sized Governments

How much government is too much, for a balanced economy? Most economists think about this question in numbers, flagging a threat to growth when the budget deficit tops 3 percent of GDP. That's a useful rule of thumb, but my approach is more holistic, looking broadly at the question of whether the state is meddling in the economy more or less.

The conventional wisdom is still that less government involvement in the economy is better for growth, and broadly I would agree. There are, however, many countries where the state is too weak even to provide the basic infrastructure necessary for growth, and for them more government would be a step forward. Successful nations don't have small governments; they have the right-sized government for their stage of development.

Government attempts to manage economic growth come in many forms, but I watch three basic trends: how the level of government spending changes as a share of GDP, whether that spending is going to productive ends, and how much the government is restraining growth in private companies or misusing state companies for political goals.

When Spending Becomes a Problem

As a country grows wealthier, spending by the government tends to increase. So, to spot nations that are out of balance, I identify those where government spending is much higher (or lower) as a share of the economy than in other nations at the same income level. The worst case is a fat state getting fatter, compared to its peers. Among the top twenty developed economies, the rotund king of this class has long been France.

The French government spends an annual sum equal to 56 percent of GDP, more than any other country, barring the possible exception of Communist throwbacks like North Korea. France's spending level is 18 percentage points above the 39 percent average* for developed nations—the biggest gap in the world. Over the last decade, the tax burden required to support this state was driving businesspeople out of the country in droves, and adding to the deep trove of French jokes about government bumbling. In the early twentieth century, France's own president, Georges Clemenceau,

---

* The norm here is defined by use of a simple regression, comparing government spending as a share of GDP to GDP per capita. Government spending data is from the IMF, which includes national, state, and local governments and defines spending broadly to include everything from the public payroll to welfare payments.

described it as "a very fertile country: you plant bureaucrats and taxes grow."[1]

Many European states have been under pressure to cut back since the crisis of 2008, particularly where their spending amounts to more than half of GDP. Led by France, that list includes Sweden, Finland, Belgium, Denmark, Italy, and until recently, Greece. Greece has been moving in a positive direction—with state spending falling from 51 to 47 percent of GDP—in part because its creditors forced Athens to make painful cuts in civil service jobs and salaries.

The downsizing of even the Greek state demonstrates that government is not fated to evolve into the Leviathan that some conservatives fear. Prior crises had already started to erode the welfare state in Europe, starting in the late 1990s in Sweden, which has since seen state spending fall from 68 to 48 percent of GDP. Germany, too, began cutting welfare benefits, and over the last decade it has lowered state spending by 3 percentage points, to 44 percent of GDP. Scarred by the crisis of 2008 and its aftermath, other European nations will remain under pressure to keep the size of the state in check.

The lighter spenders in the developed world include the United States, Austria, and Australia, with government spending amounting to between 35 and 40 percent of GDP. Switzerland was even lower, at 33 percent, in part because its pension and healthcare services are not counted as government agencies. Nonetheless, Switzerland's government is quite lean. Tax collections amount to only 29 percent of GDP—among the lowest in the developed world—

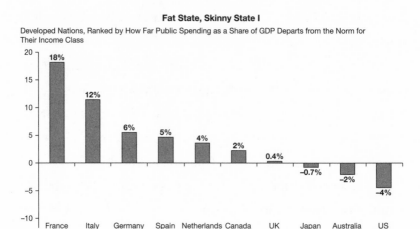

Fat State, Skinny State I

Developed Nations, Ranked by How Far Public Spending as a Share of GDP Departs from the Norm for Their Income Class

Source: Haver Analytics, IMF; data as of 2018.

reflecting a political system that decides many issues by referendum, giving Swiss voters the right to veto tax hikes and prevent bloat in their government.

Emerging Big Spenders

Among the twenty largest emerging nations, the outlier for many years was Brazil, where official government spending amounted to more than 40 percent of GDP, a level more typical of a rich European welfare state than a middle-class nation. In recent years, under a controversial right-wing government, that figure has come down to 38 percent, still well above the 32 percent average for nations with a per capita income of around $12,000. But what matters most is that the trend was moving in the right direction. Bucking the general move toward higher spending and deficits, Brazil had by 2019 fallen behind Poland (42 percent) and Argentina (39 percent) for the title of the emerging world's biggest, most bloated spender.

In emerging countries, however, these numbers have to be treated with caution. Russia, for example, reports that state spending is 33 percent of GDP, but in the past Moscow officials have admitted privately that the share is closer to 50 percent, which would make it a bigger spender than Poland.

Brazil's recent turn reflects the growing realization that it could not keep spending like a rich European welfare state, as well as growing frustration with the dysfunctional system. When millions of Brazilians joined street protests in 2013, their central grievance was that the state takes much more in taxes than it delivers in services. When the Brazilian Institute of Planning and Taxation, a consulting firm, compared government tax collection and service delivery in thirty major countries, it found the worst results in Brazil: the Brazilian government collected the most in taxes—35 percent of GDP—but ranked last in terms of delivering public services. This inefficiency is not surprising, since Brazil started building a European-style welfare state at an early stage of development, when public institutions don't have the capacity to deliver and are often corrupt.

The large emerging countries with the smallest governments include Indonesia, Nigeria, South Korea, and Taiwan, and the last two should be no surprise. The East Asian success stories were built on a model that, until very recently, delayed the development of welfare programs, kept government spending around 20 percent of GDP or less, and focused that spending on investment in infra-

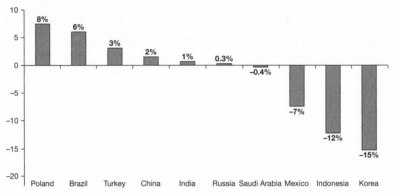

Fat State, Skinny State II

Emerging Countries, Ranked by How Far Public Spending as a Share of GDP Departs from the Norm for Their Income Class

Source: Haver Analytics, IMF; data as of 2018.

structure and manufacturing. Even today, only 30 percent of Asia's population is covered by a pension plan, compared to more than 90 percent in Europe. Taiwan's government spends an amount equal to just 18 percent of GDP, which is half the norm for its income class, and it has developed pension and healthcare systems with a careful eye to controlling costs. Its public healthcare system did not exist in 1995 but now covers nearly 100 percent of the population and costs just 7 percent of GDP; that compares well to spotty coverage costing 18 percent of GDP in the United States.

  Interestingly, Latin governments have a reputation for over-spending that is not fully borne out by the numbers. Governments in the Andean countries of Colombia, Peru, and Chile all look relatively undersized, as does Mexico, with government spending equal to 25 percent of GDP, 7 percentage points below the average for its income class. It is mainly on the Atlantic coast—in Brazil, Venezuela, and Argentina—that governments suffer from bloat.

When Government Is Too Small

The state needs to be large enough to maintain conditions essential to civilized commerce, including basic infrastructure and mechanisms to contain corruption, monopolies, and crime. An inability to collect enough taxes to support these missions suggests administrative incompetence and invites popular disdain. In Mexico, the state collects taxes equal to about 16 percent of GDP, which is quite low for a middle-class country, and it is having difficulty maintaining law and order and battling the corrupting influence of drug cartels.

In the weakest states, like Pakistan, Nigeria, and Egypt, the thin veneer of state authority creates a strange sense of fragility. Pakistan has 180 million people, but fewer than 4 million are registered taxpayers, and fewer than 1 million file taxes. The edifice of state authority is so riddled with loopholes that one almost feels it could blow apart at any moment, in some upwelling of the underserved majority.

The underbelly of the underfunded state is the black economy, where people do business off the books to evade taxes. Jobs in this netherworld tend to be poorly paid, dead-end career paths without benefits. The black economy can be shockingly large—from 8 percent of GDP in Switzerland and the United States to more than 30 percent in Pakistan, Venezuela, Russia, and Egypt. Employers in this realm get the kind of productivity they pay for.

Tax-dodging spills over into other forms of dysfunction. Nonpayers tend to avoid banks, thereby reducing the pool of savings available for investment and creating an inefficient back channel for allocating capital. It's not uncommon for Egyptians to throw fake weddings as a way to raise capital from friends and relatives, without going to the bank or paying taxes.[2]

A fragile state can face sudden pressure to raise revenue, destabilizing already unbalanced economies. When Indonesian president Joko Widodo (commonly known as Jokowi) took office in 2014, his government set out to fix crumbling bridges and roads by raising tax collections from 12 percent of GDP to 30 percent within a year. To hit that target, tax agents resorted to staking out car dealerships and real estate offices to collect on the spot. Not surprisingly, car, motorbike, and property sales slumped, and the economy slowed further. In cases like this, the basic problem is a state too weak and small to support growth.

Misreading the Lessons of China

Most of the Asian miracle economies were governed, in their early years, by autocrats. But that doesn't mean they favored big government or rigid state control of the economy. Early on, they invested almost exclusively in supporting export manufacturers, which meant building roads and factories. Welfare systems were designed to keep industrial laborers on the job. Protecting the weak was seen as the responsibility of family, not the state.

It was only after the Asian financial crisis that South Korea and Taiwan started to roll out an "inclusive" welfare system, aiming to protect the poor, the weak, and the elderly. By then they had average incomes approaching $15,000, much higher than emerging countries that began rolling out inclusive welfare systems when they were much less wealthy, such as India or Brazil. Even today, the typical East Asian government spends only about 20 percent of GDP, a pittance for relatively rich countries.

So, the East Asian model was state capitalism with a small "s," and it respected market forces. Asia scholar Joe Studwell has written that South Korea's leaders didn't pick industrial champions; they encouraged competition and then helped the winners become global players. Governments helped with financial, technical, and marketing support, but in a way, as Nobel laureate Joseph Stiglitz has pointed out, "that promoted rather than thwarted the development of private entrepreneurship."[3]

One of the biggest misconceptions about China, the most recent East Asian miracle, is that its economy took off under the rigid control of an all-powerful state. In fact, China began to grow rapidly only after the government started to ease its grip on the economy in 1980.[4]

Since the early 1980s, the output of private companies in China has risen by a factor of 300, or five times faster than the output of state companies. As a result, the share of GDP produced by state companies has fallen from about 70 percent in the early 1980s to about 30 percent now.[5] Between 1993 and 2005, Chinese state enterprises eliminated a staggering 73 million jobs, cutting those workers loose to find their way in the growing private sector.

Yet when China managed to weather the global financial crisis of 2008 relatively unscathed, by rolling out massive new spending and lending, many pundits began writing about the "rise of state capitalism." Gatherings of the global elite began to talk about how a new "Beijing Consensus," in favor of strong government guiding the economy, was replacing the old Washington Consensus, in support of free markets.

In fact, the stimulus campaign that inspired so much hype for state capitalism represented a partial reversal of China's earlier reforms. After 2008, Beijing began to direct public spending and lending to big state-owned companies, which regained momentum. Private companies were still growing faster than state companies in the 2010s, but only 4 percentage points faster, down from 12 percentage points faster a decade earlier.

Global markets were not as impressed by the alleged benefits of state capitalism as the chattering classes were. Over the next five years, the total value of emerging stock markets fell from $11 trillion to $9 trillion, *and all of that $2 trillion loss came out of state companies.* Market players were watching closely how governments were spending stimulus funds, and they saw that much of the money was going to protect jobs at inefficiently run state companies. As profitability and productivity fell, stocks in state-owned companies collapsed. China's state oil giant, PetroChina, fell from first to fourteenth among the world's most valuable companies by market cap. Apple, the private American giant, took over the top spot.

Lately, the state has been growing quickly in many nations; in the emerging world, government spending now amounts to 31 percent of GDP, on average—up from less than 24 percent in 1994. While this increase in spending by the state is in part natural, since government has grown with national wealth in all countries during the postwar era, my sense is that most countries are getting less and less economic bang for their government buck. The key to look for—at least in the current global scene—is states that are meddling less.

Spend in Haste, Repent at Leisure

Even John Maynard Keynes, the intellectual father of stimulus campaigns, saw them as emergency measures to ease recessions, not open-ended attempts to generate growth—which is what many governments attempted after 2008. In all these cases, the spending campaign did little to accelerate growth, but rang up debts that will slow growth in coming years. This is what it means to say states are "borrowing from the future."

Among the world's twenty major economies, developed nations spent a sum equal to 4.2 percent of GDP on economic stimulus in the two years after 2008. Their counterparts in big emerging nations spent much more, 6.9 percent of GDP, simply because they had the money.

Emerging nations entered the 2008 crisis with generally low levels of public debt, large reserves of foreign currency, and strong budget surpluses or at least relatively small deficits. Having money to burn, they burned it. After bottoming at 3 percent in mid-2009, the average GDP growth rate among major emerging economies hit more than 8 percent in 2010. Supporters of big government cheered this apparent success, but the bounce back was short-lived, and the average emerging-world growth rate soon fell back to 4 percent, even as deficits kept mounting. Russia spent the equivalent of 10 percent of GDP on stimulus in 2008 and 2009 alone, much of it to bail out big state firms, and got the worst result, an 8 percent contraction in output.

By early 2018, the emerging-world budget surpluses of 2007 had melted into an average deficit equivalent to 3 percent of GDP, a level that often foretells serious budget problems. And many big emerging countries were getting little return for all the money they were spending to stimulate growth in the wake of the global financial crisis.

This explosion in state spending contributed to a serious decline in productivity. In Russia, South Africa, Brazil, India, and China, a critical measure of productivity known as the incremental capital output ratio (ICOR) rose sharply. This worrisome sign meant it was taking more capital to produce the same amount of economic growth, in part because so much money was going to wasteful government projects or giveaways.

The Political Abuse of State Banks

Despite recent waves of free market reform, many banks in the emerging world are still run by the state. State banks control about a third of all banking assets in the typical large emerging economy. Countries where that share is much higher face the resulting risk, which is that politicians will meddle in the banking system to divert funds to their pet welfare projects and investment schemes. Despite the leading role that private banks often play in the lending manias that lead to financial crises, private lending by banks and in the bond markets tends to dominate healthy financial systems in normal times.

Today the state share of bank assets is 45 percent or more in

Thailand, Brazil, and China; 60 percent or more in Malaysia, India, and Russia. Nearly one-third of Russian lending is controlled by just one bank, which is run by the central bank. Twenty years after Communism fell in Russia, it is still difficult to obtain a loan to start a small business or buy a house.

When state banks mobilize lending to fight economic downturns, the effort has a disturbing tendency to backfire. By 2014, in many emerging nations, more than 10 percent of total bank loans had gone bad—meaning the borrower had not made a payment in months. In most cases, the bad-loan problem was concentrated in state banks, which had been ordered to dole out credit as part of the stimulus campaigns. These debt burdens were a big reason why, for the rest of the decade, economic growth fell well short of popular expectations across the emerging world.

Brazil offers a case study of how the political misuse of state banks can slow an economy. After President Dilma Rousseff came to power in 2010, she started pressuring banks to fight the global slowdown by lending more. Private banks resisted, but state banks did not; BNDES, the largest state development bank in the world, gave out cheap loans to virtually any company that asked. Between 2008 and 2014, state bank lending grew 20 to 30 percent a year, and the state banks' share of total lending rose from 34 to 58 percent—an expansion unmatched anywhere else in the emerging world. The result was a rapid run-up in debt, of the kind that often clogs the banking system with bad loans and can stall the economy. True to form, Brazil fell into a catastrophic recession in 2014 and has not grown faster than 2 percent in any year since.

When State Companies Become Political Tools

Governments that mobilize public banks for political ends are likely to misuse other state-owned companies too—for example, by deploying state oil, gas, or electric companies to fight inflation by subsidizing energy prices.

Energy subsidies play a major role in draining national treasuries. In the Middle East, North Africa, and Central Asia, many governments spend more on cheap fuel than on schools or healthcare. In six countries—Uzbekistan, Turkmenistan, Iraq, Iran, Saudi Arabia, and Egypt—energy subsidies amount to more than 10 percent of GDP.

Energy subsidies keep fuel prices irrationally cheap, encouraging people to burn too much fuel, accelerating climate change and discouraging investment, which leads to shortages and inflation. Fuel subsidies also tend to widen inequality in poor countries, where cars are owned mainly by the privileged. In emerging economies, more than 40 percent of the $600 billion in annual energy subsidies goes to the richest 20 percent of the population, according to the IMF. Food subsidies do not suffer the same drawback, since they do not go mainly to the rich, but rather help the poor remain active in the workforce.

Yet energy subsidies remain popular, particularly in oil-rich regions, where gasoline is often seen as a natural bounty that should be virtually free, like water. If one country is rich in oil, neighbors often expect free gas too. Oil-poor Egypt spends as heavily on energy subsidies as oil-rich Saudi Arabia—just over 10 percent of GDP.

State-owned companies are often viewed by politicians as job-creating machines. On average, in both developed and emerging countries, jobs in government and state-owned companies amount to about 23 percent of all employment, according to data from the International Labour Organization (ILO). Governments above that mark look bloated. In East Asian economies known for small government—Japan, South Korea, and Taiwan—government accounts for less than 10 percent of all jobs. In the generous welfare states of Norway, Sweden, and Denmark, government accounts for around 30 percent of all jobs. And in the bloated oil state of Russia, it accounts for 38 percent.

Since the crisis of 2008, Russia has expanded the 400,000-person payroll at Gazprom, the state-owned gas giant. In China, the state share of employment is estimated at around 30 percent, and it has been inching higher since 2008. China's state tobacco company alone employs half a million people and accounts for 43 percent of cigarette sales worldwide. The power of these behemoths is a threat to the balance of emerging economies, and scaling them back has to be a top reform priority.

The Fifty Shades of Meddling in Private Companies

What's needed is a sensible Leviathan that spends money in a strategic way and creates stable conditions in which entrepreneurial types—whether in government or private business—dare to invest.

Consider the contrast between Russia and Poland, both of which shook off Communism in the late 1980s. Poland is evolving in line with continental European powers like Germany, where the state supports the private economy with the help of clear rules.

Russia is regressing, expanding the state under regulations that shift with the whims of autocratic bosses, who have allowed and encouraged well-connected oligarchs to take over private companies, both Russian and foreign owned. This trend started in the oil patch and over the course of the 2010s spread across the economy, with state-run banks pushing out efficient foreign rivals and a state umbrella company venturing into armaments, pharmaceuticals, and other industries.

Backroom deals of this kind discourage any business activity outside the political "in" crowd. Until recently, the Kremlin elite appeared content to leave small internet industries to younger members of the wider Moscow elite. Russia was one of the few nations in which locals were holding their own—without state support— against American internet companies. By 2014, however, the Kremlin began taking steps to control internet servers and monitor traffic, and that April it transferred half the shares of a company known as the Russian Facebook to allies of Putin.

Meddling in this way kills small business. The number of companies listed on the Moscow stock exchange exploded from fewer than 50 in 2002 to 600 in 2008 but has since dwindled to fewer than 300. In contrast, Poland created fertile ground for entrepreneurs, and the number of listed companies has risen steadily from 200 in 2002 to more than 800 today.

Polish state companies are big players in industries from copper mining to banking, but they are not swallowing private rivals with help from the president's office. Instead, Poland is pushing state companies to reform. Even in unionized industries like mining, state companies have brought in professional management, cut payrolls, and raised profits, transforming themselves into legitimate global competitors.

In Brazil, the state is so bloated that there is an unusual sub-culture of companies devoted to dodging its rules. For example, a 2002 revamp of regulations set off a boom in dentistry, and Brazil now has more dental schools and more dentists per capita than the United States or Europe. Brazil has many kinds of service companies that are found in few, if any, other countries, including one that rents vehicles only to corporate clients and makes its money selling one-year-old cars. These businesses innovate in order to evade byzantine regulations, so they provide services that would serve no niche outside Brazil. This is the opposite of a society in which competitive global companies flourish under sensible laws.

A Sensible Role for the State

When commentators call for "structural reform," they are generally summoning a lesson of Econ 101: an economy's output is the sum of three basic inputs—land, labor, and capital. Structural reform often entails creating an efficient regime governing the purchase of land for new business ventures, the lending of capital to finance those ventures, and the hiring and firing of workers to staff them. In Indonesia, a recent increase in public investment was spurred by bureaucratic reforms that cut the time required to complete land acquisitions from a matter of years to days or weeks.

Though it is politically incorrect to say so, some cultures seem less eager than others to follow sensible rules. Since the early 1990s, the number of nations with a law requiring the government to run a balanced budget has risen from a handful to more than thirty—but not all take this pledge seriously. The recent battles over Greece's debt crisis pitted those who thought Athens should be compelled to respect Eurozone spending caps against those who thought it should get a pass. In Indonesia, by contrast, the Jokowi government cut spending to keep its deficit under a new legal cap, despite the resulting economic slowdown in 2014 and 2015.

India may be the world's largest democracy, but it still has a relatively loose respect for laws. Even a genteel sport like golf is played under free-flowing rules that are often debated hole by hole. In the early 2000s, India drafted a law capping the budget and aiming to keep the deficit under 3 percent of GDP, but it was ignored when the government wanted to boost spending in response to the crisis of 2008. A decade later, India has yet to hit the 3 percent target again. Where rules are often ignored, the uncertainty can distort economic outcomes.

———————

To spot whether the state is meddling more, or less, look first at trends in government spending as a share of GDP. Then check whether the spending is going to productive investment or to giveaways. Finally look at whether the government is using state companies and banks as tools to pump up growth and contain inflation, and whether it is choking or encouraging private businesses.

In recent years many countries have been raising the government share of the economy, steering bank loans to big state companies, subsidizing cheap gas for the privileged classes, and enforcing insensible rules in an unpredictable way. Even low-income countries like India are rolling out full-service welfare systems, a luxury that the Asian miracle economies began to adopt only much later in their development. At that point, countries like South Korea and Taiwan had already invested heavily in factories and transport networks, and they could well afford inclusive pension and health programs.

In contrast, many states are now managing the economy in ways that effectively retard growth, thereby fueling disrespect for establishment politicians, and the rise of radical populists. In an environment like this, especially, less meddling is best.

5

GEOGRAPHY

Successful Nations Make
the Most of Their Location

It has become fashionable to say that location no longer matters, because the internet allows anyone to provide services from anywhere. But physical goods still make up the bulk of global trade, amounting to about $18 trillion a year, compared to $4 trillion for services. Since transport is an even larger share of manufacturing costs than wages are, location near trade routes or important trade customers is still critical for makers of goods. And even service industries are not scattering to wherever there is an internet connection; they are clustering in accessible, convenient, and attractive cities.

While countries can't change their location, the most successful ones make the most of their location. To spot likely winners, I watch what countries are doing to develop trade and investment with the world, and with their neighbors. I also track what they are doing to make sure gains from growth and trade are spreading to provincial regions, and are not concentrated in a few large cities.

Nations that are successfully building trade ties to the world, and spreading the wealth to their own provinces, are carving out what I think of as a geographic sweet spot. The best current example is China. It has invested hundreds of billions of dollars to build ports on a coast largely devoid of natural harbors, to forge trade and investment ties across Asia and the world, and to transform fishing villages into globally competitive cities.

Ties to the World

It is no accident that the Asian "miracles" in Japan, South Korea, Taiwan, and Singapore sustained average annual export growth of around 20 percent—twice as fast as the average for the rest of the world—during their sustained runs of rapid economic growth. Export sales are critical to steady growth, earning the foreign income that allows a nation to invest in new factories and roads, and to import consumer goods, without building up foreign debt and sparking currency crises.

And geography is critical to exports. Any nation that wants to thrive as an export power has a huge advantage if it is located on trade routes that connect the richest customers to the most competitive suppliers.

The Hong Kong–based economist Jonathan Anderson created a "heat map" of rising manufacturing powers and found that the common link was location.[1] In recent decades, countries in which manufactured exports have grown significantly as a share of GDP have been clustered in Southeast Asia, led by Vietnam and Cambodia, and in eastern Europe, led by Poland, the Czech Republic, and Hungary. In short, wrote Anderson, they are located either next to the big consumer markets of Europe and the United States, or "on the same shipping lanes that Japan and the original Asian tigers" used to transport goods to Western markets.

Vietnam is replacing China as a base for making sneakers for export to the West. Poland is prospering as a platform for German companies to manufacture cars and other goods for export to western Europe. To a lesser extent, Mexico and Central America have also seen an increase in manufactured exports, owing in part to proximity and low shipping costs to the United States.

To get a handle on which countries are likely to thrive in export competition, the first thing I check is their location: whether they are on a critical trade route, and how open they are to global trade. Among the largest emerging nations, trade amounts to 60 percent of GDP on average, and countries well above that average tend to be major export manufacturers, led by the Czech Republic, Vietnam, Malaysia, and Thailand.

The most closed economies, with trade at less than 40 percent of GDP, fall into two groups. Populous countries like China, India, and Indonesia rely less on trade simply because their domestic markets are so large. The other group includes commodity economies like Nigeria, Iran, and Peru, which have a history of protecting themselves from foreign competition. On a list of thirty of the largest emerging countries, the most closed is Brazil, which has both a large domestic population and a commodity economy. There, trade has been stuck for decades at around 20 percent of GDP, the lowest level of any country outside deliberately isolated outliers such as North Korea. Though it is a leading exporter of soybeans and corn and has been hyped as a breadbasket to the world, Brazil has been resisting opening to the world for years. Its trade share of GDP is barely two-thirds that of peers like China, India, and Russia.

Historically, Brazil simply didn't do trade deals. By 2016, it had cut only five trade deals, all with small economies like Egypt and Israel, while India and China had both cut nearly twenty, with major economies all over the world. That cloistered mind-set began to change under President Jair Bolsonaro, who took power in 2019, but Brazil still had a long way to go. To compete in trade, a country has to show up more often at the negotiating table.

Good Luck, Good Policy

Around the year 1500, for the first time in history, the average incomes in one region—Europe—began to clearly outpace all others. And it continued to do so for the next three and a half centuries. According to development experts Daron Acemoglu, Simon Johnson, and James Robinson, the rise of Europe was driven largely by Britain and the Netherlands, which had major ports on Atlantic trade routes, as well as monarchs wise enough to respect private property rights and grant merchants the latitude to exploit growing trade channels.[2]

In short, the secret of Europe's success was the good luck of location, leveraged by good policy. That combination still works today and explains more than a few recent booms, including the comeback of Vietnam. Late in the first decade of this century, Vietnam was hyped as the next China, even though its young population was only one-tenth as large and its Communist reformers were not as competent. Vietnam ran up its debts at a rate that would normally signal a sharp economic slowdown, yet when the global credit crisis hit in 2008, the country barely stumbled.

The strongest explanation is that Vietnam was cleverly exploiting its position on key east–west trade routes. It struck a major trade deal with the United States in 2000, joined the World Trade Organization in 2007, and benefited greatly as export manufacturers started looking for alternatives to China's rising wages. After 2008, global trade was growing more slowly than the world economy for the first time in a generation, and Vietnam was one of the few emerging countries that were rapidly increasing their share of global exports.

Japanese firms cited Vietnam as their preferred site for new Asian plants, drawn in by a cheap currency, a rapidly improving transportation network, and reasonably inexpensive labor. Work was in full swing on new metro lines in Ho Chi Minh City, as well as on new roads and bridges all over the country. Vietnam was building an old-school manufacturing powerhouse, reminiscent of Japan in the 1960s, and turning itself into a new geographic sweet spot.

Ties to the Neighbors

The last round of talks on opening global trade, the so-called Doha Round, went off the rails amid the tensions of the 2008 financial crisis and collapsed in 2015. As a result, many countries are shifting focus to building regional trading communities and common markets—a promising sign.

It is natural for any nation to trade most heavily with its neighbors; in fact, postwar economic success stories have tended to cluster in regions from southern Europe to East Asia. The latter offers perhaps the most promising model. Rising intraregional trade was one of the main drivers of the long economic miracles in Japan, Taiwan, South Korea, and lately China, all of which proved willing to drop old wartime animosities to cut trade deals. In 2015, China signed a landmark free trade agreement with South Korea that was expected to inspire copycat deals across East Asia, perhaps beyond.

The biggest opportunities are in the worst-connected regions. Around 70 percent of exports from European countries go to regional neighbors, and in East Asia and North America the figure is 50 percent. In Latin America the figure is only 20 percent, in Africa it is 12 percent, and in South Asia it is just 5 percent—so these continents have the most room for regional deals to drive new growth.

Strong leadership is critical to getting deals done. Asia's postwar boom began in Japan and spread to a second tier of economies led by South Korea and Taiwan, then to a third tier led by Thailand and Indonesia, and a fourth led by China. A Japanese economist called this the "flying geese" model of development[3]—with Japan playing the lead goose.

In recent years, a similar story has unfolded in Indochina, as wealthier neighbors persuaded Vietnam, Laos, and Cambodia to drop their Communist guard and start building transport arteries that now form a network "as dense as the wiring on a computer chip," one Thai official told me.

Meanwhile, South Asia remains fenced off. Isolation, lawlessness, and the lingering bitterness produced by regional wars have made it difficult for India, Pakistan, Bangladesh, and Sri Lanka to open borders, and so far, no leader has stepped forward to ease hostilities.

Africa's record is mixed. Founded in 2000 by Kenya, Tanzania, and Uganda, the East African Community later expanded to include Rwanda and Burundi, and delivered on its aims to boost trade by building the regional roads, rails, and ports required to accelerate commerce.

Other African trade groups were stillborn. West Africa has been trying since 1975 to energize a union known by its acronym ECOWAS, built around the anchor state of Nigeria. But wars and chaos have limited its accomplishments to what has been called "organizational matters such as the drafting of protocols and the conduct of studies."[4]

South America was for decades just as sharply divided. On the Atlantic coast there is an old trade alliance, Mercosur. Traditionally hostile to free trade, it combined Brazil, Argentina, Bolivia, Paraguay, and Venezuela in what has been described as "an anti-gringo talking shop."[5] Then came the recent advent of conservative governments in Argentina and Brazil, which combined to expel Venezuela and then complete what was hailed as a landmark free trade deal with the European Union in the summer of 2019. Though trade has declined as a contributor to growth in Mercosur member states since its inception, that trend may change.

On the Pacific coast, meanwhile, there is "the most important alliance you've never heard of," as former Venezuelan trade minister Moisés Naím put it. Linking Chile to Colombia and Peru, the Pacific alliance achieved more within twenty months of its 2013 founding than Mercosur had in two decades,[6] quickly eliminating

92 percent of the tariffs among its member states, scrapping visa requirements for business travelers and tourists, and focusing on practical progress rather than bashing the United States. Building regional trade deals can be a very good sign, if it is done right.

Geography Is Not Destiny

As McKinsey & Company has pointed out, the world's "center of economic gravity"—the point most central to commercial activity—has shifted rapidly in the last half century, moving from North America over the North Pole to China, where it started out a thousand years ago.[7] This shift shows that global trade patterns do change and can be altered by smart policies.

Under strong leaders starting with Deng Xiaoping in the early 1980s, China carved out its own geographic destiny. It dredged rivers and harbors to create six of the world's ten busiest ports, all of them located on a Pacific coast with much less "prime port property" than the United States has.[8]

Now the center of economic gravity is moving again. As wages rise in China, simple manufacturing is moving, and not necessarily to countries with the cheapest labor, which counts for only 5 percent of export production costs in emerging nations, on average.[9] Instead, manufacturers are choosing countries, like Vietnam, Cambodia, and Bangladesh, that combine lower wages with a location on Pacific trade routes and open doors to outsiders.

After leaving the Indian Ocean, the major shipping routes run into the Red Sea and through the Suez Canal to the Mediterranean, where they pass states that are struggling (Libya, Sudan,

Algeria) and a few that are thriving. The relatively placid kingdom of Morocco is drawing investors with new free trade zones, a stable currency, cheap labor, and competent leadership. It is one of the first African countries to attract Western companies looking to build advanced industries such as aeronautics and automobiles.

Opportunities to extend these global trade routes abound. British colonizers first imagined a Trans-African Highway from Cairo to Cape Town, but today it is a patchwork of finished and unfinished road, with many stretches in decay or teeming with bandits. The highways from Central to South America are another tangle of more or less finished roads, interrupted at the Darien Gap, 60 miles of impenetrable rain forest on the Panama-Colombia border.

China is working to connect these less tracked regions. In 2013, Chinese president Xi Jinping began unveiling plans for a New Silk Road, evoking the land and sea routes that tied China to the West in the thirteenth and fourteenth centuries. The $300 billion plan aims to connect central China to its border provinces, and the border provinces to seaports worldwide, including those that Beijing is funding, from Gwadar in Pakistan to Chittagong in Bangladesh, Kyaukpyu in Myanmar, and Hambantota in Sri Lanka. In Europe, Poland and Hungary, among others, have already signed on as partners in the plan.

China seems to understand how to make the most of its location, and how to make sure its own provinces participate. Plans for the New Silk Road include "domestic silk roads" that will fan out from central China, turning western Xinjiang province into a transport hub for central and South Asia, Guangxi and Yunnan into hubs for Southeast Asia and the Mekong region, and Inner

Mongolia and Heilongjiang into hubs for travel north to Russia. When complete, the network could bring outposts of the old Silk Road, like the western city of Urumqi, back onto global routes for the first time since the Mongol era. This is how geographic sweet spots are developed, by spreading the wealth.

Second Cities

The need to spread a nation's rising wealth to remote provinces came home to me on visits to Thailand, where in 2010, a long simmering urban-rural conflict was erupting in Bangkok. Local experts told me that rural anger could be explained in one number: the 10-million-plus population of central Bangkok is more than ten times larger than that of the second-largest city, Chiang Mai.

A ratio that lopsided is abnormal. In small countries, it's common for the population to be concentrated in one city, but in midsize countries like Thailand, with 20 to 100 million people, and in large countries of more than 100 million and meganations of more than 1 billion, it is unusual. Typically, in midsize nations, the population of the largest city outnumbers that of the second city by around three to one, and often less. That ratio held in the past and holds today for urban centers of the Asian miracle economies, including Tokyo and Osaka in Japan, Seoul and Busan in South Korea, and Taipei and Kaohsiung in Taiwan.

My sense is that any midsize nation where this ratio is significantly more than three to one faces a risk of Thai-style regional conflict. Today, a look at the twenty major emerging economies in this population class shows that ten look out of balance, most dramatically in the cases of Thailand, Argentina, and above all, Peru. The 10.4 million residents of the Peruvian capital, Lima, outnumber residents of Arequipa, the second city, by a factor of twelve, helping to explain why Peru still faces embers of the Shining Path, a rural insurgency that raged in the 1980s.

Though Vietnam also looks out of balance on the second-city rule, it has seen little unrest as a result, because the provinces are flourishing. After Vietnam's civil war ended in 1975 with victory for the north, its leaders buried the hatchet and promoted development all over the country. Two of the world's fastest-growing ports are in Vietnam—one in southern Ho Chi Minh City, the other in the northern city of Haiphong. Between them, the old American naval base at Da Nang has tripled in population, to nearly a million, since 1975 and has been called an emerging "Singapore," with a bustling port and a streamlined local government.

Colombia is the only Andean nation with regionally balanced growth. Bogotá's 9.8 million people amount to less than three times the population of Medellín, and both Medellín and the third major city, Cali, are growing at a healthy pace. Once known as the murder capital of the world, Medellín began to turn around in the 1990s, after the central government gave local officials more control over their own budgets and police forces.

In the developed world, seven countries have a midsize population between 20 and 100 million. In five—Canada, Australia, Italy, Spain, and Germany—the first city is no more than twice as populous as the second. In the United Kingdom, where London is more than three times larger than Manchester, residents of provincial cities have long complained that national policies favor the global elite of London. Those resentments came to a head in 2016 when the provinces combined to outvote London and take Britain out of the European Union.

France is even more unbalanced. Paris accounts for 30 percent of the economy, and the 11 million Parisians outnumber residents of the second city, Lyon, nearly seven to one. In the past, France has tried to redistribute wealth to the provinces by building new towns or cutting the number of domestic regions to consolidate their political power. But Paris still dominates, and one way an economic turnaround in France will likely manifest itself is in the emergence of other large cities.

Countries with a population of more than 100 million will naturally have many big cities, so the relative size of the second city is less revealing. In these large countries, I look at the broader rise of second-tier cities—meaning cities with more than a million people.

Eight emerging countries have populations of more than 100 million but less than a billion, ranging from the Philippines with 101

The Fattest First Cities

Country	1st City Population (million)	2nd City Population (million)	Ration of 1st City to 2nd City
Peru	Lima: 10.4	Arequipa: 0.9	11.6
Argentina	Buenos Aires: 15.1	Cordoba: 1.6	9.4
Thailand	Bangkok: 10.2	Samut Prakan: 1.3	7.8
Philippines	Manila: 13.5	Davao: 1.7	7.9
Malaysia	Kuala Lumpur: 7.6	Johor Bahru: 1.0	7.6
Chile	Santiago: 6.7	Valparaiso: 1.0	6.7
France	Paris: 10.9	Lyon: 1.7	6.4
Sri Lanka	Colombo: 0.6	Sri Jayewardenepura Kotte: 0.1	6.0
Vietnam	Ho Chi Minh City: 8.1	Da Nang: 1.4	5.8
Egypt	Cairo: 20.5	Alexandria: 5.2	3.9
Kenya	Nairobi: 4.4	Mombasa: 1.2	3.7
UK	London: 9.0	Manchester: 2.7	3.3

Source: CIA World FactBook; data as of 2018.

million to Indonesia with 255 million. As countries develop, they naturally generate more second-tier cities, so it is important to compare large countries to peers at a similar level of development. Among those with a per capita income around $10,000, Russia is the laggard. Over the last three decades it has seen only two cities grow to a population of more than 1 million, compared to ten in Brazil—one of the more dynamic stories in this class. The most dynamic is Mexico, which has also produced ten cities of more than a million people since 1985, but in a national population much smaller than Brazil's.

In Mexico, second-tier cities are flowering, often as manufacturing centers producing exports bound for the United States. Among the fastest-growing Mexican cities with populations of more than a million, three are near the US border: Tijuana, Juárez, and Mexicali. In central Mexico, Querétaro is making everything from wine to appliances, and offering services from call centers to logistics. Farther south, the city of Puebla has a large Volkswagen plant. The flourishing of export manufacturing all over Mexico is a sign of unusually strong regional balance.

Until recently, the anti-Mexico was the Philippines, where the lingering influence of an old plantation society has created a remarkable split. Currently, 13 percent of Filipinos live in Manila— a proportion that has not changed since 1985 and is more than the share of people living in all other Philippine cities combined. This "missing middle" is quite unusual, even for a relatively undeveloped country like the Philippines, where average income is less than $3,000. However, second cities like Cebu and Bacolod are now growing in population, and starting to attract global call centers and IT service companies—a positive sign.

In the developed world, there are only two countries with more than 100 million people, and they are mirror opposites. Since 1985, fifteen cities in the United States have grown to more than 1 million people, compared to just one in Japan—the industrial city of Hamamatsu, southwest of Tokyo. Though second-city growth is hampered in Japan by the slow-growing national population, it is also constrained by the stagnation of Japanese policy-making, which has long favored dominant cities like Tokyo, Osaka, and Nagoya.

The United States, by contrast, is the only rich country that has seen massive internal migration, with a postwar shift of more than 15 percent of the population from the Northeast and Midwest to the South and West. People have followed the flow of companies and jobs, which have moved to younger states with lower tax rates, less heavily unionized workforces, and sunny environments made tolerable for summer office work by the spread of air-conditioning since World War II. Of the fifteen US cities that have risen into the million-plus category, thirteen are in the South or in the West— from Jacksonville, "the city where Florida begins," to Sacramento, the capital of California.

The class of meganations with more than a billion people has only two entries: China and India. And here, China is winning. It has seen nearly 100 cities grow to more than a million, twice as many as India, and has an even more dramatic lead in genuine boomtowns, cities that started out with fewer than a quarter million people three decades ago and mushroomed to more than 1 million, some many times more. There are nineteen such boomtowns in China, and only two in India—Malappuram and Kollam in Kerala state—which barely topped the million mark and only because their territory expanded when authorities redrew the local administrative maps.

In a sense, mass migration within the United States has a parallel in China, and only China, where the move has been from inland provinces to the southeastern coast. Despite China's top-down approach to growth, Beijing gave lesser cities surprising leeway to guide development, even to commandeer land for building projects. Shenzhen was a Pearl River fishing village before 1979, when Beijing made it the first of many new special economic zones, open to foreign trade and investment. The resulting boom lifted Shenzhen, as well as neighboring Dongguan and Zhuhai, and these three are China's fastest-growing cities.

In India, cities grow more slowly in part just because the economy has grown more slowly, but authorities there have also done much less to encourage second cities. India is a slow-moving democracy, where local opposition can block development and the state still reserves huge swaths of urban land for itself. Lutyens' Delhi, a verdant 25-square-kilometer enclave in the capital named after the British architect who designed it, is owned almost entirely by the government. It includes a "bungalow zone" of homes valued at up to $50 million, occupied by top officials. In the emerging world, the only comparable government oases I know of are also in India, in second-tier cities like Patna and Bareilly.

India tried to create special economic zones like China did, but it imposed restrictive rules on the use of land and labor, so these zones have done little to create jobs or build urban populations. India's outdated building codes discourage development and drive up urban prices.

Though Delhi has in recent decades ceded significant spending authority to chief ministers in India's twenty-nine states, that power has not filtered down to the mayoral level. Smaller cities struggle to grow, and when rural Indians migrate, they gravitate to one of the megacities, with populations of over 10 million: Mumbai, Delhi, Kolkata, and Bangalore. If China is a nation of boom cities, India is a land of creaking megacities surrounded by small towns, in large part because of bad policies pushed by a cumbersome state.

Firing on All Three Fronts

Location still matters. In a period when trade and capital flows have slowed, growth that once flourished along trade routes is accompanied by the rise of cities at the center of various service industries. Though the internet was expected to disperse service jobs to the far corners of the world, it has instead concentrated industries from insurance to finance in about fifty global cities, from New York and London to Shanghai and Buenos Aires. People still need to meet face-to-face to conduct business, and the result is the rise of cities with a cluster of talent in a specific service niche: Busan, South Korea, in shipping logistics; Manila in back-office services; and so on.

To carve out a geographic sweet spot, a country needs to open its doors on three fronts: to trade with its neighbors, the wider world, and its own provinces and second cities. In Asia, the leading example of a country firing on all fronts is China, with countries like Vietnam and Bangladesh close on its tail. In Latin America, the leading examples are Mexico and, of late, Colombia. The latter's

2012 free trade deal with the United States was the first of its kind in South America; Colombia belongs to one of the more promising new regional trade alliances, along with its Andean neighbors and Mexico, and it has encouraged the transformation of Medellín from murder capital to model second city. In Africa, Morocco and Rwanda are carving out export success stories in very rough neighborhoods.

Geography is never enough to produce strong growth on its own, unless a country takes steps to turn its ports and cities into commercially attractive magnets. The luck of location can change too: the advantage of a location on the border of rich markets like the United States or Germany depends on which one is growing faster at any given time. Trade routes are not written in stone, and the advantages or disadvantages of location can be reshaped by good policies. Not so long ago China was seen as hopelessly poor and isolated, before it took the steps necessary to carve out a new geographic sweet spot and put itself at the center of global trade.

6

INVESTMENT

Successful Nations Invest Heavily, and Wisely

Any economic textbook will tell you that growth can be tallied as the sum of spending by consumers and government plus investment and net exports: $(C + G) + (I + X) =$ GDP. It is one of the most basic formulas in economics, but what the book often won't tell you is why I reveals the most about where the economy is heading.

Without investment, there would be no money for government and consumers to spend. I includes total investment by both the government and private business in the construction of roads, railways, and the like; in plants and equipment, from office machines to drill presses; and in buildings, from schools to private homes. Investment helps create the new businesses and jobs that put money in consumers' pockets.

Consumption typically represents by far the largest share of spending in the economy—more than half. Investment is usually much smaller, around 20 percent of GDP in developed economies,

25 percent in developing economies, give or take.* Yet *I* is by far the most important indicator of change, because booms and busts in investment typically drive recessions and recoveries. In the United States, for example, investment is six times more volatile than consumption, and during a typical recession it contracts by more than 10 percent, while growth in consumer spending merely slows down.

In successful nations, investment is generally rising as a share of the economy. Over the long term, when investment spending reaches a certain critical mass, it tends to keep moving in the same upward direction for nearly a decade. When investment is rising, economic growth is much more likely to accelerate.

There is a rough sweet spot for investment in emerging economies. Looking at my list of the fifty-six highly successful postwar economies in which growth exceeded 6 percent for a decade or more, on average these countries were investing about 25 percent of GDP during the course of the boom. Often, growth picks up as investment accelerates. So any emerging country is generally in a strong position to grow rapidly when investment is high—roughly between 25 and 35 percent of GDP—and rising.

On the other hand, economies face weak prospects when investment is low, roughly 20 percent of GDP or less—and falling. Many countries, including Brazil, Mexico, and Nigeria, have stagnated at these low levels for years, and here the failure to invest manifests itself in a breakdown of public life: endless lines at the airline

---

* Throughout this chapter, investment as a share of GDP refers to total investment, public plus private.

ticket counter, overflowing trains with riders squatting on the top, or underpaid traffic police hitting people up for bribes.

In reaction, one often sees private citizens building their own workarounds: the private rooftop helipads that link corporate head-quarters in São Paulo, the gated communities north of Mexico City, the generators that companies use to keep the lights on during out-ages in Lagos. Much of what makes the emerging world feel chaotic reflects a shortage of investment in the basics.

In developed economies, investment spending tends to be lower because basic infrastructure is already built, so I pay less attention to the level of spending as a share of GDP and more to whether it is rising or falling. Strong growth in investment is almost always a good sign, but the stronger it gets, the more important it is to track where the spending is going.

The second part of this rule aims to distinguish between good and bad investment binges. The best binges unfold when companies funnel money into projects that fuel growth in the future: new tech-nology, new roads and ports, or—especially—new factories.

Of the three main economic sectors—agriculture, services, and manufacturing—manufacturing has been the ticket out of poverty for many countries. Even today, when robots threaten to replace humans on the assembly line, no other sector has the proven ability to play the booster role for job creation and economic growth that manufacturing has in the past.

As a nation develops, investment and manufacturing both account for a shrinking share of the economy, but they continue to play an outsize role in driving growth. Manufacturing generates around 15 percent of global GDP, down from more than 25 percent in 1970. Yet, in larger economies at all levels of development, from the United States to India, manufacturing accounts for nearly 80 percent of private-sector research and development, and 40 percent of growth in productivity, according to the McKinsey Global Institute.[1] When workers are increasingly productive, turning out more widgets per hour, their employer can raise wages without raising the price it charges for widgets, which allows the economy to grow without inflation.

As the French economist Louis Gave has argued,[2] an investment binge can be judged by what it leaves behind. Following a good binge on manufacturing, technology, or infrastructure, the country finds itself with new cement factories, fiber-optic cables, or rail lines, which will help the economy grow as it recovers. Bad binges—in commodities or real estate—often leave behind trouble.

Investment does little to raise productivity when it goes into real estate, which has other risks as well: it is often financed by heavy debts that can drag down the economy. When money flows into commodities like oil, it tends to chase rising prices and evaporate without a trace as prices collapse. So, while investment booms are often a good sign, it matters a great deal where the money is going.

The Virtuous Cycle of Investment

Nations that invest wisely tend to generate a positive economic momentum of their own. When investment surpasses 30 percent as a share of GDP, it sticks at that level for nine years, on average, for the postwar cases I have studied. Leaders in many of these nations showed a strong commitment to investment, particularly in manufacturing, which can begin a virtuous circle. Harvard economist Dani Rodrik calls manufacturing the "automatic escalator" because once a country finds a niche in global manufacturing, productivity often seems to start rising automatically.[3]

The early steps have always involved manufacturing goods for export. In a study of 150 emerging nations looking back fifty years, the Hong Kong–based economic research firm led by Jonathan Anderson found that the single most powerful driver of economic booms was sustained growth in exports, especially of manufactured products.[4] Exporting manufactured goods increases income and consumption, and generates foreign revenues that allow the country to import the machinery and materials needed to upgrade its factories, and to build roads and ports to move goods from factories to export markets, all without running up foreign bills and debts. In short, manufacturing investment seems to spark other good binges.

In the nineteenth century the United States saw two huge railroad spending booms, followed by two quick busts, but the booms left behind the rail network that would help make the country the world's leading industrial power. China began industrializing when it was still very poor, and for three decades the investment went into factories, roads, bridges, and other productive assets. Only when the boom was in its fourth decade did investment flows in China shift to frivolous targets like real estate showplaces.

There are, of course, exceptions: countries that invested heavily but so unwisely that they were left with little to show for it. In the Soviet Union, investment peaked at 35 percent of GDP in the early 1980s, but much of that money was directed by the state into ill-conceived one-industry towns, from the timber mills of Vydrino to the mines of Pikalyovo. In India, investment exceeded 30 percent of GDP during the early 2000s, but little went into manufacturing. Between 1989 and 2010, India generated about 10 million manufacturing jobs, but nearly all in small shops; investors fear building large factories, which attract tough scrutiny from bureaucrats enforcing strict labor rules.[5] The absence of large manufacturing in India is thus a symptom of the state's failure to create conditions in which business can thrive.

The Service Escalator

Before the global financial crisis, Indian economists began to argue that their country's heavy investment in technology service industries could work as a development strategy for the internet age. While Western consumers would still need a local beautician or landscaper, they could purchase many services, from law to radiology, over the internet. Instead of developing by exporting manufactured products, India could grow rich by exporting services. The idea of the new "service escalator" to prosperity was born.[6]

If only this could work. In times of technology-induced job destruction, we should be looking not for a catastrophic ending but for the next transformation. However, in the emerging world most new service jobs are still in traditional ventures like curbside bicycle repairs, or barbershops in plywood stalls. These services do not generate export earnings or boost nations up the development ladder.

In India, economists got excited about modern IT services, which had made cities such as Bangalore and Pune world-famous boomtowns. The hope was that India could advance from simple

back-office services to more profitable consulting and software services. But a decade on, India's tech sector is still focused on back-
office operations. Only about 4 million people work directly in IT,
barely more than 1 percent of the workforce.

IT service booms inspired similar hopes in Pakistan and Sri
Lanka but produced jobs in only the tens of thousands. In the Philippines, employment in call centers and other back-office services
exploded from no jobs in the early years of this century to more than
a million by 2018, but people who land these jobs are often already
middle-class and well-educated urbanites who speak English.

Lately, in emerging countries, service industries have not risen
fast enough to drive mass modernization of the labor force, the way
manufacturing did in the past. In Japan and South Korea, as much
as a quarter of the population migrated from farm to factory during their long periods of "miracle" growth. At the peak of its manufacturing prowess in the early postwar years, the United States
employed one-third of its labor force in factories. Workers can move
quickly from farms to assembly lines, because both rely on manual
labor. The leap from the farm to modern services—which require
advanced language and computer skills—is tougher. For now, the
rule still looks for investment in factories first.

The Narrow Ladder to a Stable Perch

It is getting harder for established export manufacturers just to hold
on to their customers, in part because the sector has been shrinking
worldwide. Exports out of the big emerging economies had been
growing at an annual pace above 20 percent before the global finan-

cial crisis of 2008, with peaks near 40 percent. But then global trade slowed, and export growth in these nations turned negative by the middle of the next decade.

As the manufacturing sector shrank, competition intensified. New players like Vietnam and Bangladesh rose up to challenge China, and rich countries began moving to block the tricks (subsidizing exports, undervaluing currencies) that East Asian nations had used to become export powerhouses in the 1960s and '70s.

Developed nations, led by the United States, also began adopting advanced manufacturing techniques, and they built a huge lead in this field. As both competition and protectionism spread, manufacturing hubs in the developed world are reviving as major rivals for emerging-world factories, and the manufacturing ladder is getting tougher for any developing country to climb.

Historically, the clearest measure of success has been the pace at which a country is increasing its share of the global market for manufactured exports. Recent successes include China, Thailand, and South Korea, which illustrate how strength in manufacturing can insulate an economy from shocks. In recent years, strong manufacturing has continued to drive the South Korean economy forward at a healthy pace, despite a huge burden in household debt, equal to 150 percent of GDP.

Thailand is an even more striking example. It invests a healthy 25 percent of GDP and has the second-biggest manufacturing sector (near 30 percent of GDP) among large economies. It has been increasing its share of global manufactured exports, including steel, machinery, and cars, and as a result Thailand has an unusually high proportion of adults who are gainfully employed. They act as ballast, stabilizing the economy even when protestors are filling the streets.

Thailand has suffered thirteen coups and a further six coup attempts since the 1930s. Yet before the last coup, in 2014, Thailand had sustained an economic growth rate of around 4 percent for a decade. Even in late 1997, when the Bangkok real estate market was crashing, Japanese companies were powering an investment boom on the eastern seaboard, where new auto and petrochemical plants were rising on green, pagoda-dotted hills and white-sand beaches. This investment binge helped Thailand bounce back much faster after the crisis than most people expected.

The Upside of Tech Booms

After the dot-com crash of 2001, the conventional wisdom was that tech investment bubbles fuel mainly junk companies. While hundreds of companies went under in 2001, a few, including Google and Amazon, would survive to help make the United States much more productive. In fact, the dot-com boom helped to drive the US productivity growth rate up from 2 percent in the 1980s to near 3 percent in the 1990s, the highest rate since the 1950s.[7]

Even though the tech boom imploded, it left consumers with the ability to make phone calls and transfer data more cheaply, as well as to make use of call centers and other cost-effective services located in countries such as India or the Philippines, thus improving standards of living in both rich and poor countries. At the height of the dot-com mania, the huge investment in fiber-optic cables looked like the biggest bubble of all. But those cables eventually made high-speed broadband connections a reality in the United States.

The infrastructure left behind by investment binges in factories or technology tends to increase productivity for years after the boom has ended. The rub: tech booms are rare outside the leading industrial nations. In the emerging world, they have unfolded so far only in Taiwan, South Korea, Israel, and, most spectacularly, China. Recent visitors are dazzled by the most sweeping consumer tech revolution ever seen, anywhere in the world.

Land with an Indian passport and the scanner speaks to you in automated Hindi. Check into a prototype hotel with no clerks— only a scanner that recognizes you as the person who booked the room. Open your room with no key—just your face. Go to lunch at a new grocery store where your meal is delivered by little white robots rolling along a sparkling white track. Be sure to download a digital payment app, because many stores no longer take cash or credit cards. Forecasters who once questioned whether China could develop beyond low-end manufacturing have their answer.

A New China, led by the tech sector, has emerged with stunning speed as a global competitor or leader in industries ranging from renewable energy to e-commerce and artificial intelligence, and has kept up the momentum by rapidly expanding its spending on research and development. Over the last decade China's spending on R&D tripled, to around $380 billion, putting it ahead of Europe and closing the gap with the United States. In fact, the boom in tech helps explain why China's record debts, which are concentrated in old state-run industries, have slowed the economy but not led to a collapse of the economic model. The millions of jobs lost in heavy industries have been partially offset by millions hired as ride share drivers and other tech service workers.

Taiwan and South Korea have also invested heavily in research and development—more than 3 percent of GDP a year over the past decade—in order to create technology industries from scratch. South Korea has built the most complete broadband coverage in the world and is globally competitive in industries from cars to consumer electronics. Taiwan's companies are quick to respond to new global trends but so far have been confined mainly to making components for PCs, mobile handsets, and other consumer electronics.

Israel also fostered a tech boom while it was still developing. Israel is home to the second-highest number of start-up companies in the world, after the United States, and spends nearly 4 percent of GDP on R&D. Several large US corporations, such as Microsoft and Cisco, set up their first overseas R&D facilities in Israel, and the country now derives 40 percent of its GDP from exports and half of its export income from tech and life sciences.

Another possible tech binge is unfolding in Mexico, where the Monterrey Institute of Technology now plays a role similar to that played by Stanford University in Silicon Valley, a cornerstone of a local culture that celebrates engineering, entrepreneurship, and aggressive innovation. Today, Monterrey is home to a striking array of companies that are applying high technology to everything from lightweight aluminum auto parts to white cheese and cement.

Elsewhere, trend watchers have spotted new Silicon Valleys popping up from Nairobi, Kenya, to Santiago, Chile, but often these are microbooms, consisting of a few individual start-ups in one small neighborhood. Chile spends less than 1 percent of GDP a year on research and development—a fraction of what Asian rivals spend, and not enough to drive a real tech boom.

Bad Binges: Real Estate

The worst investment binges leave behind little of productive value, in part because the trigger is not a real innovation but spiking prices for a coveted asset like real estate or oil. Investors pouring money into houses may accelerate construction—not a bad thing—but a house will provide a home to one family, not a steady boost to productivity. And since so many people dream of buying that perfect home, the real estate market seems particularly prone to irrational manias and runaway debts.

The quality of an investment binge also depends on how businesses pay for it. If they borrow money, trouble erupts when the bubble bursts. As businesses and banks struggle to deal with bad debts, the credit system is paralyzed and the economy slows for years.

But if businesses raise money by selling equity shares, the market sorts out the mess. Stock prices fall, and owners are forced to take the hit; there is no protracted negotiation. The best funding source is foreign direct investment, because when foreigners buy direct stakes in businesses, they tie themselves to these projects as owners. This financing can't flee easily in a crisis.

Nations often move from good to bad binges, and back. In the United States, for example, the dot-com boom was a classic good binge. Because it was financed mainly by the stock market and venture capitalists, there was no debate about who should take the pain when stock prices collapsed. The United States fell into recession, but it was the shallowest in postwar history, and it left some valuable investments behind.

The subsequent boom in US housing, however, was a bad binge financed largely by debt. Real estate crashed in 2008, followed by the sharpest recession in postwar history and an agonizingly slow recovery, as banks and their customers struggled to resolve the debts.

Real estate binges are often pumped up by borrowing and, as a result, tend to end in a serious economic slowdown. Some of the most famous economic miracles ended with the implosion of a debt-fueled property bubble, including Japan in 1989 and Taiwan in the early 1990s. It is hard to pinpoint when a real estate boom becomes a bubble, but a study of eighteen of the worst housing price busts since 1970, from the United States to China, suggests a rough rule of thumb: all those busts came after investment in real estate construction reached an average of about 5 percent of GDP.

It's not clear why "safe as houses" ever came to mean completely safe, since housing binges are particularly dangerous for the economy.

Bad Binges: The Curse of Commodities

Bad binges can also flow from the "curse" of natural resources. When nations discover oil or gems, a scramble over the profits ensues, corrupting the business culture and the political system. The government starts relying on oil profits, not taxes, for revenue, undermining the relationship between voters and elected leaders. To buy voters off, leaders begin subsidizing gas, cheap food, and other freebies.

Foreigners pump in money to buy the oil, which drives up the value of the currency, in turn making it difficult for local factories to export their goods. The oil windfall tends to undermine every industry other than oil, retarding development.

To study this effect, I looked at average real income in eighteen large oil-exporting nations since the year they started producing oil. In five of them, average incomes had actually fallen. And in all but one of them, Oman, average income had fallen compared with the leading global economy, the United States. Two of the largest exporters—Saudi Arabia and Russia—are not included in the chart here, for lack of income data going back to the year they discovered oil. But in recent decades they have shown a similar pattern, rising

Finding Oil, Falling Behind

Some top exporters have seen incomes drop, and all but one dropped relative to the United States, since discovering oil.

	Nation	GDP per Capita Today	$ Gain/Loss in GDP per Capita since Discovery of Oil	% Gain/Loss in GDP per Capita Relative to U.S. since Discovery of Oil
1	Oman	$18,082	$16,333	19.0%
2	Dem. Rep. of Congo	$495	-$250	-2.6%
3	Chad	$888	-$19	-2.7%
4	Sudan	$728	-$607	-4.2%
5	Syria	$2,807	$1,022	-4.5%
6	Nigeria	$2,233	$958	-5.2%
7	Angola	$3,060	$1,950	-5.5%
8	Ecuador	$6,155	$5,281	-5.9%
9	Libya	$6,836	$4,900	-6.4%
10	Cameroon	$1,538	-$703	-6.6%
11	Colombia	$6,681	$5,718	-6.7%
12	Tunisia	$3,073	$854	-6.8%
13	Republic of Congo	$2,444	$1,291	-6.8%
14	Yemen	$919	-$1,392	-9.5%
15	Algeria	$4,230	$2,511	-9.7%
16	Venezuela	$2,724	$1,655	-16.2%
17	Gabon	$8,031	$4,204	-22.6%
18	UAE	$39,806	$16,626	-133.2%

Source: Haver Analytics; data as of 2019.

and falling with oil prices, never gaining steadily on the United States in per capita income terms.

Consider what was really happening during Africa's widely hyped "renaissance" in the last decade. Many African countries grew rapidly, and investment rose from 15 to 22 percent of GDP, on average, but much of the money flowed into services and commodity industries. Manufacturing shrank as a share of Africa's exports, and millions of Africans moved out of industrial jobs and into informal shops. And while manufacturing was helping to stabilize countries like Thailand, heavy investment in commodities was destabilizing countries like Nigeria.

The largest economy in West Africa, Nigeria, has seen average income fall from 8 to 4 percent of the US average since it started pumping oil in 1958. Billions of oil dollars have disappeared into corrupt pockets.[8] With little revenue left to build roads, Nigeria struggles to attract investment. Manufacturing is less than 5 percent of GDP—the fourth lowest in Africa. The result is a deep vulnerability to outside shocks. Unlike the situation in Thailand, a currency collapse in Nigeria provides no significant boost to manufactured exports because, for the most part, they don't exist.

When Oil Economies Work, Briefly

On my list of fifty-six countries that saw at least a decade of rapid growth, twenty-four are commodity economies, including Brazil and Indonesia. But these gains were often fleeting. Over the last 200 years, the average price of commodities has remained flat in inflation-adjusted terms. Upswings tend to last for a decade, but then prices drop and stay low for around two decades, leaving the economy no richer.

In Saudi Arabia, average incomes have swung wildly with oil prices, doubling to $20,000 as oil prices shot up in the 1970s and early '80s, falling to $10,000 in the 1990s, recovering in the next decade to $25,000, and drifting back down as low as $20,000 in recent years. Countries with natural resources less bountiful than Saudi Arabia's have tended to stagnate at a much lower income level. Argentina, Colombia, Nigeria, and Peru have experienced an even more pronounced roller-coaster ride since 1960, seeing average incomes swing with prices for their commodity exports.

Though commodities are not generally an advantage in the long term, they can drive good runs of a decade or less. If the money is going mainly to a new technology, for example, investment in a commodity can qualify as a good binge. The recent shale energy boom in the United States, which was built on technology for drawing oil and gas from shale rock, forced older companies to lower prices. This cheap energy made the US economy more competitive and created a reservoir of new expertise. Just as the dot-com boom had done, the shale bubble left behind a valuable industrial infrastructure that will continue boosting productivity long after the boom is over.

The Point of Excess

While rising investment often augurs well, any strength taken too far can become a weakness—which is why the ideal level of investment is roughly in the range of 25 to 35 percent of GDP.

The Asian miracles showed that investment spending tends to be "monophasic," meaning that once trends turn, the same conditions persist for years. After investment peaks at more than 30 percent of GDP and begins to fall, it tends to keep falling. The landscape is littered with idle or unfinished plants, malls, and other ill-conceived investment projects that weigh on the economy, and growth slows by a third, on average, over the next five years.

If investment peaks at more than 40 percent of GDP, the backlog of unnecessary projects is even longer, and growth slows by about half over the next five years. Only ten countries have reached this peak in the postwar era, including South Korea in the 1970s, and Thailand and Malaysia in the 1990s. Of these countries, just two—Norway in the late 1970s and Jordan after the year 2000—escaped a major slowdown.

This signal bodes ill for China, where between 2002 and 2017, investment rose from 37 percent of GDP to 47 percent, a level never before attained by a large economy. As investment in heavy industry climbed, China was pouring better than two times as much cement per citizen as any other country. And as investment to GDP rose, more of the money started going to wacky real estate projects and the like.

When Good Binges Go Bad

China's experience is typical. In the late stages of a good boom, the number of opportunities to invest in high-return factories or technologies will diminish before the optimism does. The general euphoria makes many people complacent, and more investment goes to waste. Investors start putting money into houses, stocks, or commodities like oil and gold, and the binge starts to go bad. The economy slows because the contribution from productivity falls.

This process of decay has led to many a real estate bubble, including those that popped across Europe and the United States in the early years of the twenty-first century and the one that threatened China by the mid-2010s. By 2013, investment in real estate had risen from 6 percent of GDP to 10 percent in just five years, and the price of land had risen 500 percent since the year 2000. In major Chinese cities, prices for pre-owned homes were rising much faster than average incomes were, feeding middle-class resentment of those who could afford a house.

Since investments are often funded by borrowing, investment and credit tend to grow in tandem, and to turn for the worse together. In the 2010s, China was seeing more investment go to wasteful targets, and more financing come from debt. China's size tends to produce larger-than-life tales, and the term *ghost town* fails to capture the scale of its vacant and debt-fueled megaprojects. Outside the city of Tianjin, developers were building a financial district designed as a larger replica of New York—with a skyline one critic called "eerily similar."

As good investment binges decay, a meltdown often follows. Even in resilient Thailand, optimism about the manufacturing-driven boom inspired many locals to borrow heavily to buy real estate, inflating the bubble that collapsed in 1997.

In Malaysia, investment peaked in 1995 at 43 percent of GDP, the second-highest level ever recorded in a large economy, behind China today. Guided by an autocratic prime minister, Mahathir

Mohamad, the country poured money into some projects that proved useful, like a new international airport, and many that did not. Mahathir's grand vision included a new government district called Putrajaya, which today is home to just a quarter of the 320,000 people it was designed to house. This is another classic case of a bad binge that left behind little of value.

The Opposite of a Binge Is the Blahs

If investment is too low as a share of GDP, around 20 percent or less for emerging countries, and stays low for a long period, it is likely to leave the economy full of holes—unpaved roads, drafty schools, ill-equipped police—that make rapid growth unlikely.

Weak investment tends to degrade both the supply network and respect for the government. In African countries, including Nigeria, city dwellers often string up wires to draw free electricity from power lines, reducing revenue that the state utility needs to build out the national grid. When it rains in São Paulo or Mumbai, traffic screeches to a halt because the sewers overflow.

If a nation's supply chain is built on inadequate road, rail, and sewer lines, supply cannot keep up with demand, which drives up prices. In this way, weak investment is a critical source of inflation— a cancer that has often killed growth in emerging nations.

This link between weak investment and weak growth is clear because it is so common. In the postwar era, few countries have maintained a high rate of investment and thus generated strong GDP growth for a decade or more. Many have seen investment remain below 20 percent of GDP for a decade, and most of these

(60 percent) have seen the economy grow at a paltry rate of less than 3 percent over that decade.

Investment is the critical spending driver of growth, and a high and rising level of investment is normally a good sign. My research shows that investment running below 20 percent of GDP foretells of shortages and gridlock; above 40 percent is excessive and often presages a serious slowdown. The sustainable sweet spot for investment is between 25 and 35 percent of GDP, and it can last for many years, particularly if the investment is going to projects that generate growth in the future.

The most productive investment binges are in manufacturing, technology, and infrastructure, including roads, power grids, and water systems. The worst are in real estate, which often rings up crippling debts; and commodities, which often have a corrupting influence on the economy and society.

Although a case can be made that services will come to rival manufacturing as a catalyst for sustained growth, that day has yet to arrive. For now, the best investment binges are still focused on manufacturing and technology.

7

INFLATION

Successful Nations Control
the Real Inflation Threats

No subject in economics is more paralyzed by traditional thinking than *inflation*, a term that generally refers only to the pace of increase in consumer prices, a once ubiquitous threat that has largely vanished in recent decades.

Consumer prices were rising at a double-digit pace and wreaking economic havoc all over the world until the early 1980s, when they began to recede under pressure from rising global competition and a concerted attack by central banks. Raising interest rates to painful heights, central banks choked off money flows and won the war on inflation just about everywhere. Between 1981 and 1991, the average rate of inflation in developed nations fell from 12 percent to just 2 percent, where it remains today.

Meanwhile, in emerging nations, the average rate of inflation peaked at a staggering 87 percent in 1994 and reached the hyperinflationary triple digits in major countries like Brazil and Russia. Then, over the subsequent decades, it receded to its current, much calmer rate of just 4 percent.

Those averages are still very useful as benchmarks for judging when inflation may be too high. Any emerging nation with a rate of inflation much above 4 percent, or any developed nation with a rate much above 2 percent, has cause for concern. In a world where double- and triple-digit consumer price inflation is a rare threat, the outliers are worth watching closely because they are out of balance and seriously at risk.

The traditional view of high consumer price inflation—that it is a growth-killing cancer—still holds true. In the short term, rapidly rising prices compel central banks to raise interest rates, making it more expensive for businesses and consumers to borrow. High inflation also tends to be volatile, and its swings make it impossible for businesses to plan and invest for the future. Over the longer term, inflation erodes the value of money sitting in the bank or in bonds, thus discouraging saving and shrinking the pool of money available to invest in future growth.

The rub is that central banks are now fighting a very different war. In the slow-growth environment that took hold after the crisis of 2008, central banks often worry that inflation may be too low, not too high. In developed countries, instead of raising rates to make sure inflation doesn't increase to far above a target of 2 percent, they now cut interest rates when inflation is falling too far below 2 percent. Their big fear is that low inflation will lead to outright deflation—the dreaded but overblown "Japan scenario."

History, in fact, shows that neither low inflation nor deflation are necessarily bad for economic growth. Japan suffered a rare bout of "bad deflation" after the collapse of its stock and housing bubbles in 1990. Consumer demand dried up, prices started to fall, and shoppers began delaying purchases in the expectation that prices would fall further. The downward spiral depressed growth for two decades. However, deflation can also follow a new tech or financial innovation that lowers production costs and boosts economic growth.

If inflation is too high, it is almost always a threat to growth, but the same cannot be said of low inflation. Even if low inflation threatens to devolve into deflation, it could be good for growth if falling prices are driven by new innovations and expanding supply, rather than by depressed demand.

Perhaps the deepest flaw in traditional thinking, however, is that it still focuses on the kind of inflation that has largely disappeared. After central banks won the war on high consumer price inflation, they cut interest rates to levels that have fueled a massive run-up in prices for financial assets, including stocks, bonds, and houses. And in recent decades, as we have seen, stock market and housing bubbles have been increasingly common precursors to financial crises and recessions.

Economists have been very slow to recognize this new inflation threat, and central banks have been very slow to think outside their official mandates, which focus on stabilizing the economy by controlling inflation in consumer prices, only. But successful nations will control both kinds of inflation, in consumer markets and in financial markets.

Hot Economies Don't Run High Inflation

Textbook economics typically traces consumer price inflation to unpredictable demand shocks (like spikes in government spending or consumer euphoria) or supply shocks (like oil price hikes and droughts). In practice, however, countries make themselves vulnerable to inflation when they invest too little in roads, communications, and other supply networks. If these networks are inadequate, supply will fall short of demand, and prices will begin to rise very early in an economic recovery, ensuring that it won't last long.

A classic case is Brazil, where (as we have seen) investment has stagnated for decades at around 20 percent of GDP. The government has invested too little in roads, schools, and public infrastructure of all kinds, so when economic activity starts to pick up, companies quickly begin bidding up prices for a limited supply of everything from transport services to skilled employees. As a result, prices begin to rise at a very early stage in the economic cycle.

Because Brazilians have come to expect large price increases early in a recovery, they are also quick to demand higher wages. Inflation thus begins to raise its ugly head at a GDP growth rate of 4 percent or even less, forcing the central bank to increase interest rates and restrain economic growth. Brazil has thus inadvertently built a high-inflation economy, in which growth tends to sputter out before it really gets going.

This is the opposite of what happens in an economy headed for a long boom. On my list of the fifty-six nations that, since 1960, have posted runs of GDP growth faster than 6 percent for at least a decade, nearly three out of four had inflation rates lower than the emerging-world average during those runs.

The thirteen best-known postwar miracle economies typically invested the equivalent of 30 percent of GDP every year, and high growth was accompanied by low inflation. South Korea, Taiwan, Singapore, and China all saw booms lasting three decades or more, and rarely saw inflation higher than the emerging-world average. In some miracle cases, inflation was high at the start of the boom but fell gradually. Moreover, one of the signs heralding the end of these growth "miracles" was a flare-up in inflation, like sparks from a sputtering engine.

In China, investment peaked at 47 percent of GDP in 2011, and much of it was, until recently, flowing into new roads, phone networks, and factories. Now, when the economy starts to pick up, businesses can put half-idle factories and railcars back on a full schedule, so there is no upward pressure on prices. During China's long boom, lasting three decades through 2008, its extensive supply networks made it possible for the economy to grow at 10 percent with an average inflation rate of around 5 percent. That is a record any emerging country would die for.

Inflation and the Circle of Life

There is never one cause of a political revolt, but food prices have played a role in many. Consumer prices have thus been intimately connected to the cycle of political crisis, revolt, and reform described in chapter 2.

Though the Revolutions of 1848 targeted European monarchies and followed the spread of democratic ideas on the continent, new research identifies spiking food prices as the main catalyst.[1] In recent decades, Latin America has been a cauldron of inflation-driven unrest. Between 1946 and 1983, according to Martin Paldam of Aarhus University in Denmark, 15 governments fell in Latin America, and in 13 of those cases, from Mexico to Argentina, the regime change followed a surge in the annual rate of consumer price inflation to 20 percent or more.[2] Rising prices for wheat and other grains also contributed to the 1989 fall of Communism in the Soviet Union.

In the following decade, inflation fell in most emerging nations, but occasional flare-ups continued to topple leaders. University of Minnesota economist Marc Bellemare found a strong link between food prices and unrest in many countries between 1990 and 2011.[3] Inflation helped oust regimes in Brazil, Turkey, and Russia (again) in the late 1990s. In 2008, World Bank president Robert Zoellick warned that at least thirty-three countries faced a risk of social revolt sparked by food prices, which had risen 80 percent in the previous three years.[4]

In fact, food prices did help spark revolts worldwide in 2011, including the Arab Spring. Yet in India, where rising prices for staple foods have been toppling leaders since British rule, out-of-touch leaders of the ruling Congress Party continued to argue that inflation was no cause for worry. While I was traveling through India before the seminal 2013 election, all I heard from voters was complaints about the price of onions. After Congress lost, and Narendra

Modi's Hindu nationalist party took over, polls showed that inflation had played a major role in the government's downfall.

The point is that high or rapidly rising consumer price inflation threatens economic growth directly and indirectly, because it
can provoke destabilizing social protest. So, watch for leaders who
understand this inflation threat, and how to use the weapons that
can control it.

Weapons against Consumer Price Inflation

In part, the victory over consumer price inflation was won by opening to global trade. The world is much more interconnected now
than it was before China and other emerging nations began to open
to trade around 1980, and despite a recent slowdown, trade with
these low-cost countries continues to restrain both wages and prices
for consumer goods worldwide. If local wages rise, producers can
shift operations to countries with lower wages. If a local supplier
raises prices, wholesalers can just find a cheaper supplier overseas.
Opening to these global market forces maintains a permanent
check on inflation.

The second weapon against consumer price inflation is sound
financial management. In the late 1990s, as we have seen, a new
generation of leaders, with Kim Dae-jung of South Korea at the
forefront, brought a new ethos of financial responsibility to the
emerging world. These leaders began stealing less, keeping budgets
in balance, and investing more wisely, including in supply networks.

Perhaps the most important weapon is held by central banks.

For much of the postwar era, even many nominally independent central banks could not ignore pressure from political leaders, who generally pushed for low interest rates and easy money, even with inflation threatening. But the crises of the 1970s showed leaders how painful inflation can be, particularly for poor and middle-class voters, and turned many politicians into anti-inflation warriors.

That shift in attitude freed central banks to fight inflation in earnest. The revolution began in New Zealand, which passed a law in 1989 that granted its central bank independence and directed it to set a target for inflation. Critics screamed that the move could destroy jobs, and one offered to supply a rope to hang central-bank chief Don Brash, but the measure passed. Having seen his uncle's life savings wiped out by inflation, Brash declared that fighting inflation would be the bank's top priority, and within two years the inflation rate fell from nearly 8 percent to hit the new target: 2 percent.[5]

Inspired by Brash, central bankers in Canada, Sweden, Britain, and beyond soon began to apply inflation targets. Citigroup estimates that fifty-eight countries (including the Eurozone members as one country), accounting for 92 percent of global GDP, now have an inflation target. Emerging countries, including Chile, Brazil, Turkey, and Russia, adopted targets, which proved effective if the central bank managed to change expectations—to convince the public it was prepared to increase the price of money and induce the pain necessary to control inflation. Even in inflation-prone Brazil, the central bank adopted a tough target in 1999, and inflation fell to just 4 percent over the next seven years, after averaging in the high triple digits for a decade.

This struggle is far from over, however. The legal independence of central banks is honored strictly in emerging countries like South Africa, Chile, Poland, and the Czech Republic, but not so much in others. Though officially committed to targeting inflation, many central banks are still informally obliged to answer the phone when the president's office calls asking for easy money. To figure out whether a nation has the tools to fight inflation, look first for a genuinely independent central bank, and next, for a clear inflation target.

Good and Bad Deflation

The problem with targets is that trying to hit them makes more sense when consumer price inflation is high and rising than when it is low and falling, as is increasingly the case.

To reconstruct price trends before official records began in the twentieth century, investigators turn to government surveys, farm ledgers, even department store catalogs. The earliest records are available in only a few developed countries, starting with Britain and Sweden, and thus "global" measurements likely become less accurate as researchers push back in time, but the broad trend is clear. For the eight centuries beginning in 1210, the world's average annual inflation rate was only 1 percent, according to the Global Financial Database.

For most of that period, however, the long-term 1 percent average concealed sharp swings between inflation and deflation. Then, in the early 1930s, deflation disappeared (see the chart), for reasons that remain mysterious but include the spread of the banking industry and the wider availability of credit, with consequently more money chasing the available goods. The end of the gold standard in the 1970s made it easier for central banks to print money, which also tends to fuel inflation. The result was that deflation disappeared completely on the global level, and bouts of deflation—particularly longer ones—became much less common within individual nations as well.

A Deutsche Bank analysis showed that before 1930, it was common for more than half of all countries to be experiencing deflation in any given year. After 1930 it was rare for even one country in ten to be experiencing deflation. In the postwar period, only two economies have experienced deflation lasting at least three years: the little-known case of Hong Kong—for seven years after 1998—and the infamous case of Japan after its bubble burst in 1990.[6]

The Japan case gave deflation its bad name. After Japan's housing and stock market bubbles burst in the early 1990s, demand fell

The 800-Year History of Inflation

Global Year-over-Year Median Inflation

Source: Global Financial Database, using a sample of 30 countries; shown as a five-year moving average.

and prices started to decline, as heavily indebted consumers began to delay purchases of everything from cars to TV sets, waiting for prices to fall further. The economy slowed to a crawl. Hoping to jar consumers into spending again, the central bank pumped money into the economy, but to no avail. Critics said Japan took action too gradually, so its economy remained stuck in a deflationary trap for years.

After the crisis of 2008, many countries seemed to face a combination of forces similar to what triggered deflation in Japan, including heavy debt and supply overcapacity. By 2015, with inflation dropping close to zero in developed nations, the fear was that other countries could fall into a deflationary spiral like Japan's.

Deflationary spirals are hard to stop because of the effect on consumers, and on debtors as well. As prices fall, every unit of the local currency is effectively worth more, and hard-pressed borrowers are forced to pay down loans in an increasingly valuable currency. As the American economist Irving Fisher put it during the Great Depression, "The more debtors pay, the more they owe."[7] The deflationary spirals that struck Japan and Hong Kong were sustained in part by strong currencies and mounting debt burdens.

The problem, however, is that not all deflationary cycles are destructive. In *The Great Wave*, Brandeis University historian David Hackett Fischer traced the records for the United States and various European countries as far back as the eleventh century and found long periods when stable or falling prices were accompanied by high GDP growth.[8] In these periods, the fall in prices was not driven by a blow to consumer demand.

These waves of good deflation all date from before the 1930s, and they were driven by technological or institutional innovations that lowered the cost of producing and distributing consumer goods. Holland's economy tripled in size during the seventeenth century as new openings to trade and innovations in finance sparked a golden age of inflation-free growth. In England in the late eighteenth and early nineteenth centuries, breakthroughs such as the steam engine, railroads, and electricity were lowering the costs of making everything from flour to clothing. During this era, consumer prices fell by half, while industrial output rose sevenfold. In the United States during the early 1920s, the economy was expanding at a near 4 percent pace annually, and new labor-saving devices such as the truck were driving down prices for consumer goods from food to home furnishings.

The point is that one can't say consumer price deflation is in itself good or bad for growth. Between the late 1870s and the outbreak of World War I in 1914, the US economy grew at a steady average pace of around 3 percent. During the first half of this period, deflation averaged 3 percent a year, and during the second half, inflation averaged 3 percent a year.

Though deflation has largely vanished, worldwide, it continues to surface in isolated pockets. Japan is the only major country to have suffered a multiyear case of deflation in the postwar era, but many countries have suffered a single-year bout. Again, however, these periods did not have a consistent impact on growth, for better or worse.

In early 2015, the Bank for International Settlements (BIS) looked at the postwar record for thirty-eight countries. In all, these countries had seen more than 100 years in which prices fell. On average, GDP growth was higher by a statistically insignificant margin during deflationary years, at 3.2 percent, than during inflationary years, at 2.7 percent. The cases in which deflation was accompanied by strong growth occurred from Thailand and China to the Netherlands and Japan. The BIS concluded there is no clear evidence that consumer price deflation is bad—or good—for economic growth.[9]

But how can you tell when consumer price deflation is the good kind, driven by growing supply, or the bad kind, driven by shrinking demand? This task requires parsing conflicting forces of supply and demand, often with unclear results. The takeaway is simply that while many analysts now assume that any hint of deflation is worrisome, this assumption is not borne out by the evidence. High inflation for consumer prices is almost always a threat to growth, but deflation is not.

Consumer Prices Aren't the Whole Story

Central bankers and economists still tend to focus on consumer price inflation, even though it has largely disappeared, and to ignore prices for assets like stocks, bonds, and real estate, even though there is an increasingly clear link between real estate and stock market busts and economic downturns.

Rising global competition and the emergence of independent central banks have helped countries contain consumer prices. But globalization is pushing asset prices in the opposite direction. In a world with few barriers to the flow of capital, foreigners are often the main buyers of stocks, bonds, and real estate in markets from New York to Seoul, making prices for these assets less stable, and an increasingly telling signal of a coming economic crash.

Research by the International Center for Monetary and Banking Studies shows that many postwar economic "miracles," ranging from Italy and Japan in the 1950s to Latin America and Southeast Asia later, first took off because of strong fundamentals (like strong investment and low inflation) but were sustained by rapidly rising debts and ended with a bursting property bubble.

In recent decades, recessions have been more likely to originate in debt-fueled property booms, for the simple reason that there has been an explosion in mortgage finance. As Alan Taylor has pointed out, since the boom in modern finance began in the late nineteenth century, mortgage lending has grown much faster than other lending to households and private companies, which helps explain why economic booms and busts "seem to be increasingly shaped by the dynamics of mortgage credit."

The growing threat posed by asset bubbles was dramatized in a 2015 paper by Taylor and his colleagues, who researched 170 years of data for seventeen countries.[10] Before World War II, there were 78 recessions—including only 19 that followed a bubble in stocks or housing. After the war, there were 88 recessions, the vast majority of which, 62, followed a stock or housing bubble.

For the last three decades, every major economic shock has been preceded by a bubble in housing, stocks, or both, including Japan's meltdown in 1990, the Asian financial crisis of 1997–98, the dot-com crash of 2000–2001, and, of course, the global financial crisis of 2008.

Often, a crash in prices of houses or stocks will depress the economy, by making people feel suddenly less wealthy. Thus shaken, they spend less, resulting in lower demand and a fall in consumer prices. In other words, asset price crashes can trigger bouts of bad consumer price deflation.

This is what happened in Japan, where the real estate and stock crash of 1990 led to the long fall in both asset and consumer prices. It also happened in the United States, where the stock crash of 1929 was followed by consumer price deflation in the early years of the Great Depression.

But how can you identify potentially threatening asset price bubbles? Be alert when prices are rising at a pace faster than underlying economic growth for an extended period, particularly for housing. While home prices typically rise by about 5 percent a year, the IMF has found that this pace speeds up to between 10 and 12 percent in the two years before a period of financial distress.[11]

Taylor and his team added a useful warning: once prices for stocks or housing rise sharply above their long-term trend, a subsequent drop in prices of 15 percent or more signals that the economy is due to face significant pain. In general, they found, housing bubbles were much less common than stock bubbles but were much more likely to be followed by a recession.

The downturn is much more severe if borrowing fuels the bubble. When a recession follows a bubble that is not fueled by debt, five years later the economy will be 1 to 1.5 percent smaller than it would have been if the bubble had never occurred. However, if investors borrow heavily to buy stock, the economy five years later will be 4 percent smaller. If they borrow to purchase housing, the economy will be as much as 9 percent smaller.

It is time for forecasters, including those at central banks, to recognize that times have changed. In a globalized world, with few barriers to capital flows, investors around the world can bid up prices for stocks, bonds, and real estate in local markets from New York to Shanghai. Central banks have fueled these purchases with record low interest rates and by entering the bond market as major buyers themselves. Largely as a result, global financial assets (including only stocks and bonds) are worth $280 trillion and amount to about 330 percent of global GDP, up from $12 trillion and just 110 percent in 1980.

Traditionally, economists have looked for trouble in the economy to cause trouble in the markets. They see no cause for concern when loose financial policy is inflating prices in the markets, as long as consumer prices remain quiet. Even conservatives who worry about easy money "blowing bubbles" still look mainly for economic threats to the financial markets, rather than the threat that overgrown markets pose to the economy. But financial markets are now so large that the tail wags the dog. A market downturn can easily trigger the next big economic downturn.

———

The general rule is that strong growth is most likely to continue if consumer prices are rising slowly, or even if they are falling as the result of good deflation, driven by a strengthening supply network. But in today's globalized economy, in which cross-border competition tends to suppress prices for consumer goods but drive them up for financial assets, watching consumer prices is not enough. Increasingly, recessions follow instability in the financial markets. To understand how inflation is likely to impact economic growth, you have to keep an eye on stock and house prices too.

8

CURRENCY

Successful Nations Feel Cheap

Political leaders often celebrate a strong currency as the sign of a strong economy, overlooking the risks. If a currency starts appreciating too fast, foreigners will start buying local stocks or bonds not because they believe in the economy, but because they believe the rising currency will increase the US dollar value of those investments. For a while this bet is self-fulfilling, as foreign money continues to drive up the value of the local currency. Eventually, though, an expensive currency makes the country's exports too pricey to compete in global markets. The economy stalls, the currency crashes, and the country will be poised to grow only when it stabilizes again, at a competitive value.

Ironically, successful nations feel cheap, at least to foreign visitors. Cheap is good because a currency that makes local prices feel affordable will draw money into the economy through exports, tourism, and other channels. An overpriced currency will encourage both locals and foreigners to move money out of the country, eventually sapping economic growth.

In many countries, nonetheless, politicians still ascribe a weakening currency to nefarious plots, as King Henry I did. In 1124, suspicious that conniving royal money changers were to blame for the falling value of the English sterling, he summoned them to Winchester and, in what historian Nicholas Mayhew described as "a very public occasion designed to bolster confidence," subjected the entire lot to castration or, for the less unlucky ones, amputation of the right hand.[1] Today, the understanding of currency movements has advanced a little, but perhaps not as much as you might expect.

Why "Feel" Is the Best Measure

Judging a currency by how cheap it "feels" may sound vague, but there is no better way. If it takes three Brazilian reals to buy a dollar today and four reals next year, it appears that one real is buying less and less. But that is not necessarily the case, if prices are rising at different rates in the United States and Brazil.

To accurately value currencies, one has to correct for different inflation rates. One common measure, the real effective exchange rate (REER), corrects for consumer price inflation in a country's major trading partners. Competing measures correct for producer prices, labor costs, or per capita income. The results, however, are often contradictory. The Brazilian real may look cheap by one measure, expensive by another, fairly priced by a third. As a veteran analyst once put it to my team, "In valuing currencies, nothing works."

To improve clarity, experts have attempted to rank how expensive countries are by comparing prices for common items. The granddaddy of these rankings is the *Economist*'s Big Mac index, but others compare prices for Starbucks coffee, iPhones, and other goods. All these approaches acknowledge that the only way to value a national currency is by how cheap it feels to buy goods in that country.

The more formal measures are open to manipulation by politicians, who can make their currency, and thus their country, look competitive by cherry-picking data. The Turkish lira looks a lot less expensive when compared to its high price in the 1970s than to its cheap price in the 1990s. In the absence of an accurate measure, outsiders need to trust that they will know an expensive currency when they feel it.

Of course, the feel of a currency will vary with the traveler. Brazil may feel less expensive to Americans paying in dollars than to Europeans paying in euros. In general, though, a rising currency tends to be rising against most major currencies, and the currency that matters most is the US dollar.

Why the Dollar Matters Most

Even though the United States has slipped as an economic superpower—it accounts for 24 percent of global GDP, down from a peak of 34 percent in 1998—it is still the sole financial superpower.

The world is on a dollar standard, and in some ways the reach of the dollar is expanding. When individuals and companies borrow from lenders in another country, they increasingly borrow in dollars, which now account for 75 percent of these global flows, up from 60 percent just before the global financial crisis in 2008. Even though the crisis began that year in the United States, American banks dominate global finance more now than they did before the crisis—in part because debt troubles have dogged banks in Europe, Japan, and China even more persistently.

The share of countries that use the dollar as their main "anchor"—the currency against which they measure and stabilize the value of their own currency—has risen to 60 percent today from about 30 percent in 1950. And those countries collectively account for some 70 percent of global GDP. In other words, most of the world chooses to live in a dollar bloc. And because the Federal Reserve controls the supply of dollars, it is, now more than ever, the central bank of the world.

Nearly two-thirds of the $12 trillion of foreign exchange reserves held by central banks around the world is held in dollars, and that proportion has barely changed for decades. Going back to the mid-fifteenth century, in fact, only six countries have enjoyed this "reserve currency status," and all were imperial powers, starting with Portugal, then Spain, the Netherlands, France, and Britain. All enjoyed what the French have called the "exorbitant privilege" of borrowing cheaply abroad and living well beyond their means, since every nation is happy to collect interest in the reserve currency. Americans still enjoy that luxury today.

According to the Bank for International Settlements, close to 90 percent of all global financial transactions conducted through banks use the dollar on one side, even if the deal does not involve an American party. A South Korean company that sells smartphones to Brazil will likely request payment in dollars, because most people still prefer to hold the world's leading reserve currency. In a world still dominated by the dollar, the most important perspective on any currency is how cheap it feels in dollars.

How to Read Money Flows

If the currency feels cheap and the economy is healthy, bargain hunters will pour money in. If the currency feels cheap but money is still fleeing, something is wrong. For example, in late 2014 the Russian ruble collapsed because of the falling price of oil, but Russians were still pulling tens of billions of dollars out of the country every month, fearing that the situation would get worse. Cheap was not yet a good sign, because the ruble was not yet cheap and stable.

All the legal channels for money flows can be found in the balance of payments, particularly the current account. Composed mainly of net trade (exports minus imports), the current account also includes other foreign income—remittances from locals working abroad, international aid, and interest payments—that can make import bills easier or harder to pay.

The current account thus captures how much a nation is producing compared to how much it is consuming, and it reveals how much a nation has to borrow from abroad to finance its consumption habits. If a country runs a sizable deficit in the current account for too long, it is going to amass obligations it can't pay. The trick is to identify the tipping point.

In a paper written in 2000, economist Caroline Freund found that signals of a turn for the worse flash when the current account deficit has been rising for about four years and hits a single-year peak of 5 percent of GDP. At that point, typically, businesses and investors lose confidence in the economy and start pulling out money, thus undermining the currency and forcing locals to import less. The economy slows significantly until falling imports bring the current account back into balance.[2]

Pushing Freund's research forward, I screened the available data for 186 nations going back to 1960. Testing for various sizes of deficits, over various time periods, my search[*] confirmed that when the current account deficit runs persistently high, the normal outcome is an economic slowdown. If the deficit averages between 2 and 4 percent of GDP each year over a five-year period, the slowdown is relatively mild.

If the deficit averages 5 percent or more, the slowdown is sharper, shaving an average of 2.5 percentage points off the GDP growth rate over the following five years. There are only forty cases of a current account deficit rising that fast and long; 85 percent of those cases ended in a major growth slowdown over the next five years, and 80 percent led to a crisis of some kind.[†] The growth slowdown hit countries rich and poor, including Norway and the Philippines in the 1970s, Portugal and Malaysia in the 1970s, Spain and Turkey during the last decade.

---

[*] I focused only on large economies because the current account in smaller ones can swing sharply with one big investment from abroad, skewing the results. *Large* is defined as an economy representing at least 0.2 percent of global GDP, which in 2015 was an economy of more than $150 billion.

[†] I say "of some kind" because this definition includes banking, currency, inflation, or debt crises as defined by Carmen Reinhart and Kenneth Rogoff. Data on these kinds of crises is available for 34 of the 40 cases, and 31 of them, or 91 percent, suffered at least one of these crises.

This is the danger zone: if a country runs a current account deficit as high as 5 percent of GDP each year for five years, it is consuming more than it is producing and more than it can afford. Running sustained current account deficits of more than 3 or 4 percent of GDP can also signal coming economic and financial trouble—just less urgently. In fact, some emerging-world officials have come to believe that when the current account deficit hits 3 percent of GDP, it is time to restrain consumer spending and prevent the country from living beyond its means.

Below the 3 percent threshold, a persistent current account deficit may not be a bad thing. If money is flowing out of the country to import luxury goods, which do not fuel future growth, it will be harder for the country to pay the import bills. If it is going to buy imports of factory machinery, the loans financing those purchases are supporting productive investment in future growth.

One quick way to determine whether the rising deficit is a bad sign is to check whether investment is rising as a share of GDP. Such a rise at least suggests that the money is not flowing out for frivolous consumption.

Anatomy of a Currency Crisis

Thailand offers a classic case study in how an overpriced currency allows a country to live beyond its means, driving up the current account deficit and ending in a severe economic slowdown.

In the early 1990s, Thailand saw itself as the next Japan. It had already graduated from making textiles to manufacturing cars and semiconductors, and Thais were getting too confident. Because the value of the baht was pegged to the strong US dollar, Thais felt like kings of the mall when they traveled abroad.

During this period, Thais could borrow more cheaply in dollars than in baht, and they started taking out dollar loans to buy stocks, real estate, and luxury goods. Thai bankers became known for their taste in Château Pétrus wines and Audemars Piguet watches. Property and stock prices began shooting up to heights that could last only as long as the strong baht did.

Trouble signs appeared in 1993, when China devalued its currency to boost exports at a time when its economy was weakening. The devalued renminbi helped China to gain global export market share from Asian rivals, including Thailand. Nonetheless, Thais continued consuming blithely; between 1990 and 1994 the current account deficit exploded as a share of GDP by an average of 7 percentage points a year.

Then, in the spring of 1995, the dollar started to appreciate, and the baht rose with it. The baht started to feel very expensive, slowing Thai exports. The current account deficit widened to 8 percent of GDP in 1995 and 1996, moving from deep to deeper in the danger zone.

Investors began to question Thailand's ability to pay its foreign bills and to sustain the exorbitant prices in the Bangkok stock and housing markets. When they started to pull money out, the Thai central bank responded by spending billions of dollars to buy baht, hoping to prevent a precipitous collapse. As its foreign exchange reserves dwindled, the central bank had to give up the fight and abandon the dollar peg. The baht fell 50 percent against the dollar in 1997, and suddenly Thai borrowers couldn't pay the dollar loans they had taken out to buy houses and stock.

The stock and real estate markets plummeted. In the midst of one of the worst debt binges ever recorded in the emerging world, Thailand was forced to seek a bailout from the IMF in order to pay off its foreign loans. Within months, excesses that had been mounting for years unraveled completely. As the late MIT economist Rudiger Dornbusch put it, crises "take a much longer time coming than you think, but happen much faster than you would have thought."[3]

Anatomy of a Currency Contagion

A current account deficit becomes a clear concern when it has been rising as a share of GDP for many years and the accumulated bill grows too big to pay. Yet time and again, the world has been gripped by currency contagions, in which investors start pulling money out of one troubled country, triggering a pullout from countries in the same region or income class, even though those nations can pay their bills. In a way, the serial crises that have rocked the emerging world since the 1970s are one rolling crisis built on the recurring fear that poor nations won't have the money to pay their bills. The Mexican peso crisis of '94 begat the Thai crisis of '97 begat the Argentine crisis of 2002 and many others.

At the first signs that one emerging-world currency is faltering—as the Thai baht did in 1997—investors often flee from emerging markets in general. They do not pause to distinguish between countries that face a serious current account deficit problem and those that do not.

To cite just one example, the contagion that swept emerging markets in the summer of 2013 made no distinction between the real trouble in Turkey and the passing problems in India and Indonesia. At that point, India and Indonesia were running current account deficits ranging between 2 and 4 percent of GDP, but all it took was a 10 to 20 percent fall in their currencies to quickly narrow the deficits, in part because their currencies did not feel too expensive to begin with. These countries were much less vulnerable than Turkey or Brazil, where the currencies felt very expensive and thus were likely to encourage more people to shop and invest overseas, and make a persistently large current account deficit even bigger.

Investors fled blindly from all these countries, even though Turkey was the only one seriously at risk. Its economy is almost purpose-built to run up large deficits in the current account. Located on terrain devoid of natural resources, Turkey has to import oil, iron, copper, and most other raw materials. Turks are also heavy importers of goods from cars to computers, and they save just 15 percent of their income, the lowest savings rate among large emerging countries. That means Turks have to borrow heavily from abroad to finance their consumption.

The small pool of savings starves local industries, including exporters, of investment funding. With weak exporters and heavy demand for oil and other imports, Turkey is prone to running up deficits in the current account. By 2013, it was the only major country in the world that had been running a current account deficit that averaged more than 5 percent of GDP for the previous five years. Since then it has experienced a major economic slowdown, just as this rule predicts.

Does Deglobalization Change the Rule?

To pay their import bills, countries need foreign currency, which they can obtain from foreign bank loans, foreign purchases of stocks or bonds, or direct foreign investment in local factories. These flows all show up in the capital account of the balance of payments, but analysts and newspaper headlines tend to focus only on foreign purchases of stocks and bonds—often called "hot money" because foreigners looking for a quick profit can dump stocks and bonds like hot potatoes when crises begin.

In recent decades, however, the most volatile capital flows have actually been bank loans, which are now the real hot money. After China and other emerging markets began opening their doors to foreign capital, capital flows rose from 2 percent of global GDP in 1980 to 16 percent—a whopping $9 trillion—by early 2007.

Then came the 2008 crisis, and optimism about emerging nations vanished; by 2014, capital flows had fallen back to $1.2 trillion—once again about 2 percent of current global GDP. Bank lending, the largest portion of capital flows, turned negative during the crisis, indicating that banks were liquidating loans to bring money home.

This "deglobalization of banking"[4] will make it increasingly difficult for many countries, including the United States and Britain, to continue living beyond their means by borrowing from foreigners. With capital flows slowing, these countries may run into trouble financing their persistent current account deficits much sooner. In the pre-2008 era, the tipping point came when the deficit had been increasing by 5 percent of GDP for five years in a row. In the postcrisis era, the tipping point may come faster and at lower deficit levels; the 5 percent rule may become a 3 percent rule.

Follow the Locals

When a currency crisis begins, blame often falls on big global players like hedge funds and venture capitalists for fleeing the country. This suspicion has arisen in every currency meltdown from the Asian financial crisis of 1997–98—which Malaysia's Mahathir Mohamad pinned on "evil" foreign speculators—to the 2013 attacks on the Turkish lira and other emerging currencies.[5]

The problem with these conspiracy theories is that foreigners are not more flighty or less loyal than locals. My data for twenty-one big emerging countries shows that locals have been moving money out of emerging stock markets since records begin in 1995. Local investors were net sellers in the local stock markets every single year, while foreigners were net buyers every year, with only three exceptions: 2008, 2015, and 2018.

Blaming rich foreigners for emerging-world currency crises also assumes—incorrectly—that money flows naturally from rich countries to poorer ones. Nobel laureate Robert Lucas pointed out three decades ago that it most certainly does not.[6] In financial markets, American and European investors have an incentive to seek high returns in hot emerging countries, but investors from emerging nations have an incentive to diversify by seeking safer investments—such as US Treasury bonds—in developed markets.

People move money out of self-interest, not to prove their patriotism or to sabotage foreign nations.

In fact, balance-of-payments data shows that in ten out of the twelve major emerging-market currency crises over the past two decades, local investors headed for the exits before foreigners. As the value of the currency reached its low point, foreigners did move much larger sums than locals, but they began moving later. During Mexico's "tequila crisis" in December 1994, locals started to switch out of pesos and into dollars more than eighteen months before the sudden devaluation. Similarly, locals began to pull money out of Russia more than two years before the ruble collapsed in August 1998.

Capital flight begins with locals, I suspect, because they have local intelligence. They can pick up informal signs—struggling businesses, looming bankruptcies—long before big foreign institutions do. Instead of anticipating crises, foreigners tend to sell at the bottom and lose a fortune. In eight out of the twelve major currency crises, foreigners started pulling out—calling in loans and dumping stocks and bonds—as the currency was hitting its low point.

Savvy locals are also often the first to return. In seven of the twelve major emerging-world currency crises, locals started bringing money back home earlier than foreigners and acted in time to catch the currency on its way up. Big global players are not the all-seeing eyes, and locals are not the provincial dupes, that many people seem to imagine.

As locals begin sending money abroad, it will show up in the balance of payments as capital outflows. To cite one example, outflows from Russia reached $150 billion—more than 8 percent of GDP—in 2014, the year oil prices collapsed and took the Russian economy with it.

Rich locals can also slip money out through illicit channels that show up only in the "errors and omissions" column of the balance of payments. When money flows out of Russia as "errors and omissions," money tends to flow into Britain via the same channel.[7] And the very rich often pick up and move themselves, not just their money. The research group New World Wealth, which tracks migration among the world's 15 million millionaires, found that by 2017, the largest exoduses were out of Turkey, Venezuela, India, and Russia, which lost 2 percent of its millionaire population that year alone.

Even locals who lack access to the flight paths used by the superrich always have an escape hatch. When trouble looms, Indians convert rupees into the traditional safe haven of gold, sometimes at the rate of tens of billions of dollars each quarter. In 2017, as growing financial instability sent inflation into the double digits in Turkey, ordinary Turks started converting their bank deposits from liras into dollars, effectively shipping their savings out of the country without leaving town. Meanwhile, more than one out of every ten Turkish millionaires moved out of their home country that year alone.

This was not the first time that locals successfully anticipated an important shift. Before the crises of the 1990s, domestic investors moved large sums out of emerging nations, fleeing regimes prone to seizing wealth and economies destabilized by high inflation. Since many governments strictly limited capital flows, locals often found roundabout paths that registered only as "errors and omissions."

As calm returned after 2000, locals were first to move back. They brought billions of dollars home to Indonesia, South Africa, Brazil, and other emerging nations, again often through back channels. In 2002, global markets avoided Brazil for fear of its radical new president, Lula, but locals looked past his rhetoric and saw the moderate reformer he would be in office. Their heavy purchases of reals helped stave off a currency collapse, and foreshadowed the economic rebound that followed.

To anticipate a currency crisis or recovery, follow the locals.

When Money Flows Flash a Green Light

The clearest sign that a currency crisis is about to pass comes when the current account rebounds from deficit into surplus. Such a surplus shows that the currency is likely stabilizing at a competitively low rate, boosting exports while forcing locals to cut back on imports. The country is living within its means. The crisis is passing, putting the economy in position to start growing again.

Consider how quickly Asia recovered from the crisis of 1997–98, and how slowly southern European countries recovered from the crisis that started in 2010. In Asia, the hardest-hit stock markets fell by an average of 85 percent; in Europe, they fell by an average of 70 percent. In 1997–98 the hardest-hit economy was Turkey, in 2010 it was Greece, and both saw GDP shrink by about a quarter. So the economic losses were very similar (see the chart).

Mirror Damages: Crises in Asia and Europe

Maximum Decline in Real GDP, Measured
in Local Currency, at the Depth of the Crisis

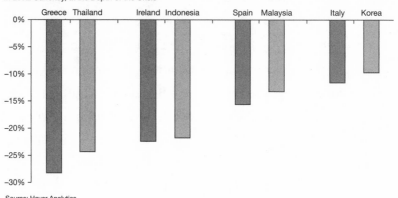

Source: Haver Analytics.

But the European recovery was slower, because the way Europe managed its currency prevented the current account from rebounding quickly from deficit into surplus.

Before their crises, both Asia and Europe adopted a fixed exchange rate in some form. Asian countries pegged the value of their currencies in dollars. Europe adopted the euro, so countries like Germany, France, and Italy no longer had a national currency, or the flexibility to allow (or manage) its value to adjust for local conditions.

In both Asia and Europe, as confidence in the new fixed currencies spread, banks lowered borrowing costs, and locals started borrowing heavily to shop, build houses, and start businesses. This spending drove current accounts into the red, stirring fears about whether these countries could pay their mounting debts.

In Asia, however, as soon as countries stopped trying to defend the dollar peg, currencies crashed. In Thailand, the epicenter of the

Asian crisis, the economy stalled, the unemployment rate tripled, property prices fell by half, and the collapsing baht reduced average income by more than a third in dollar terms. Yet within eighteen months, the cheap currency was driving a strong recovery.

The collapsing currencies forced locals to buy fewer imports and boosted exports. Current account deficits in the hardest-hit countries—Thailand, Indonesia, Malaysia, and South Korea—quickly gave way to an average surplus equal to 10 percent of GDP. Within just three and a half years, these economies recovered all the output they had lost since the massive recession started in 1998.

In Europe, however, the main crisis-hit nations could not just abandon the euro, so there was no sudden drop in the value of the currency, and no rapid drop in imports or boost to exports. The only way they could regain a competitive position was by making painful cuts to wages, welfare, and bloated public payrolls. Economists call this belt-tightening process "internal devaluation," which unfolds much more slowly and painfully than currency devaluation. Four years after the crisis, Europe's hardest-hit economies—Greece, Spain, Italy, Portugal, and Ireland—were only starting to show real improvement in the current account, and they were still struggling to recover.

Put simply, governments that attempt to create artificial stability by fixing the price of their currency tend, instead, to provoke much worse currency crises. As foreigners start to follow locals out the door, the central bank often spends billions buying its own currency, draining the national reserves but achieving only a temporary pause in the currency's slide. That pause gives investors a chance to flee the country with partial losses. Many currency traders joke that "defending the currency" really means "subsidizing the exit" of foreign investors.

You Can't Devalue Your Way to Prosperity

Since a cheap currency is an advantage in global competition, it might seem smart for national leaders just to devalue the currency. Indeed, technocrats often do order currency devaluations. But this is a form of state meddling that has proved increasingly ineffective.

Since the crisis of 2008, many nations have tried to improve their competitive position by devaluing currencies, but none have managed to gain an advantage. The central banks of the United States, Japan, Britain, and the Eurozone have pursued policies that effectively amount to printing money, in part as a way to devalue their currencies. But each has achieved at best a brief gain in export share, because rivals quickly match each other's policies. The rise in 2016 of Donald Trump, who keeps a hawkish watch on the moves of foreign central banks, made it increasingly difficult for any nation to devalue its currency without being called to account for it.

By 2019, many emerging countries had seen sharp currency depreciation, but with little boost to growth. One reason was foreign debt; since 1996, in the emerging world, the debt owed by private companies to foreign lenders had more than doubled as a share of GDP, reaching 20 percent or more in Taiwan, Peru, South Africa, Russia, Brazil, and Turkey. For these countries, devaluation made it more expensive for private companies to service foreign debt, and forced them to spend less on hiring workers or investing in new equipment.

The world had watched this self-defeating cycle before. The Latin American crisis of the 1980s began in part because Argentina, Chile, and Mexico had opened up to foreign loans, which produced sharp spurts of growth, but only briefly. Many leaders tried to revive growth by devaluing their currencies, but instead pushed many of their countrymen into default on foreign loans. The process hit bottom in Argentina, which in 2002 suffered the largest sovereign debt default in history.

Another factor that can derail devaluations is heavy dependence on imported food and energy. In this case, a cheaper currency will make it more expensive to import these staples, driving up inflation, further undermining the currency, and encouraging capital flight. This is a recurring syndrome in nations like Turkey, which imports all its oil, but the problem is spreading.

These days, even manufacturing powers are mere cogs in a global supply chain, relying heavily on imported parts and materials. They thus find it harder to capitalize on a cheap currency, because devaluation raises the prices they pay for those parts and materials.

This brings us back to China in 1993, and one of the rare devaluations that worked. China had little foreign debt, it did not rely too heavily on imported goods, and its already strong manufacturing sector grew faster after Beijing devalued the renminbi. But this was an exception that proves the rule; in general you can't devalue your way to prosperity.

Moreover, devaluation is increasingly less likely to work, even in China, which has grown to command 13 percent of global exports, the largest share any economy has reached in recent decades. It is simply too big to expand much further, and if it does devalue, others retaliate. In late 2015, China devalued the renminbi by 3 percent, and many emerging nations responded immediately, erasing any competitive gain that Beijing hoped to achieve.

China is also making increasingly advanced exports, which are less price sensitive and gain less from a cheap currency. In the 1970s and '80s, Germany and Japan enjoyed long runs of strong growth, despite massive appreciation in their currencies, not least because their customers were willing to pay more for quality goods "made in Germany" or "made in Japan." A similar evolution is under way in Korea, Taiwan, and China, where technology and capital goods make up a rising share of exports. The more advanced the economy, the less of a boost it gets from devaluations.

The feel of the currency is the simplest real-time measure of how effectively a country can compete for international trade and investment. If a currency feels too expensive, a large and sustained increase in the current account deficit can result, and money will start to flow out of the country. The longer and faster a current account deficit expands, the more risk there is of an economic slowdown and a financial crisis. Traditionally, that warning light flashed when the current account deficit had been growing at an average rate of 5 percent of GDP for five years. But the recent deglobalization of banking has made it more difficult to finance current account deficits, so the new red line may be around 3 percent.

To spot the beginning or the end of currency trouble, follow the locals. They are the first to know when a nation is in crisis or recovery, and they will be the first to move. If the local millionaires are fleeing, so should you.

Once a crisis begins, watch for the current account to bounce back to surplus, which usually means that a cheap currency is drawing money back into the country. It helps if the financial environment is stable, underpinned by low expectations of inflation, which further encourages investors to return.

If the government tries to artificially cheapen the currency, markets are likely to punish this meddling, particularly if the country has substantial foreign debt or does not manufacture exports that can benefit from a devaluation. Cheap is good only if the market, not the government, determines the feel of a currency.

9

DEBT

Successful Nations Avoid Debt Mania (and Phobia)

In recent decades, every new crisis seemed to hatch a new way of thinking about debt, and there are thousands, depending on who is lending, who is borrowing, for how long, and many other factors. Mexico's "tequila crisis" of the mid-1990s started with short-term bonds, so explanations focused on the dangers of short-term debt. The Asian financial crisis started with debt to foreigners, so foreign loans became the new obsession.

But as that crisis approached in 1997, a brusque bank analyst named Robert Zielinski had already begun to zero in on what was later revealed as the best predictor of these meltdowns: five straight years of rapid growth in private-sector debt. In October of 1997, with the crisis already ravaging Thailand, Zielinski laid out his story in a three-page play, *The Kiss of Debt*. Set in an unnamed Southeast Asian country, it describes how everyone from the prime minister to farmers gets swept up in the mania for cheap loans. A housewife borrows to invest in "four million of anything." Each step of the way, a chorus sings: "Kiss of debt, kiss of debt."

A decade later, after the global financial crisis, the Bank for International Settlements,[1] the IMF,[2] and other international authorities began to look at the same question and came up with the same basic answer as Zielinski. The most consistent precursor of major credit crises going back to the "tulip mania" in seventeenth-century Holland was that private-sector debt—borrowing by corporations and individuals—had been growing faster than the economy for a significant length of time.

The authorities also reached another surprising conclusion: the clearest signal of coming trouble is the pace of increase in debt, not the size of the debt. Size matters, but pace matters more. Government debt plays a role but usually rises later, after trouble starts in the private sector. A sharp increase in private debt is the leading indicator.

The key issue is whether debt is growing faster or slower than the economy. A country in which private credit has been growing much faster than the economy for five years should be placed on watch for a sharp slowdown in the economy and possibly for a financial crisis as well.

By 1997, private debt amounted to 165 percent of GDP in Thailand, but debts of that size would not necessarily have signaled a crisis if the debt had not been growing at an unsustainable pace. Over the previous five years, private debt had been growing at an annual pace more than twice as fast as the roaring Thai economy, and had risen by 67 percentage points as a share of GDP. To anticipate coming trouble, that is the number to watch: the five-year increase in the ratio of private credit to GDP.

Successful nations avoid debt manias and are often best positioned for sustained growth after a period of retrenchment. The upside of the rule is that if private credit has been growing much slower than the economy for five years, the economy could be headed for recovery, because banks will have rebuilt deposits and will feel comfortable lending again. Borrowers, having reduced their debt burden, will feel comfortable borrowing again.

That's the normal cycle anyway. After particularly severe credit crises, lenders and borrowers may be paralyzed for years by debtophobia, which can be almost as destructive as debt mania.

The Point of No Return

My research over the past decade pushes the post-2008 findings forward in two ways. It identifies a tipping point, past which private credit has risen so fast that a financial crisis (like a collapse in the stock market or currency) is very likely. It also shows that, beyond the tipping point, the economy is virtually certain to suffer a sharp economic slowdown—even if there is no financial crisis.

Looking back to 1960 for 150 countries, I isolated the 30 most severe credit binges, from Japan in the 1980s to Thailand and Malaysia in the late 1990s. For these cases, private credit grew over a five-year period by at least 40 percentage points as a share of GDP.[*]

---

[*] In most of these cases, GDP growth was strong during the five-year period when credit was growing dangerously fast, so credit growth was the main reason the credit/GDP ratio was rising.

In 18 cases, the country went on to suffer a financial crisis within the next five years.*

And in all 30 cases, the economy suffered a slowdown after the increase in private credit hit the 40-percentage-point threshold. On average, the GDP growth rate fell by more than half over the next five years. This 30-for-30 result is unusually consistent, and hints at what may be a law of economic gravity, at least based on patterns in national economies over the last fifty years.

Below the 40-percentage-point threshold, the decay produced by excessive debt growth is a progressive disease. If private credit grew by 25 percentage points as a share of GDP, the annual GDP growth rate slowed by a third over the next five years. If private credit grew by 15 percentage points as a share of GDP over five years, the slowdown was milder, with the annual GDP growth rate falling by 1 percentage point.

The Private Sector Leads

The investigations since 2008 have illuminated why financial crises tend to start with private companies and individuals.[3] Typically, some new innovation persuades people that the economy is entering a period of rapid growth. In the United States, credit booms have been triggered by the invention of the diving bell, the opening of canals and railroads, the advent of television and fiber-optic net-

---

* Here I use *financial crisis* to mean a banking crisis as defined by Carmen Reinhart and Kenneth Rogoff in *This Time Is Different* (2009), which captures bank runs that force a government to close, merge, bail out, or take over one or more financial institutions.

works, and the introduction of home equity loans—lending tools that allow people to borrow against the value of their homes.

As new innovations boost growth, incomes rise and people feel more confident borrowing. But this cycle of optimism can continue long after the impact of the innovation has worn off. Many businesses will keep borrowing to buy into the hot new thing, past the point justified by underlying demand. Assuming the economy will boom indefinitely, others start borrowing to build homes and offices.

When debt is growing significantly faster than the economy, even well-run banks start making mistakes, doling out loans too fast. The errors grow as dodgy private lenders get in the game, extending credit to increasingly ill-qualified borrowers—those amateurs described by Zielinski, like the housewife ready to borrow to invest in "four million of anything." When economic growth is powered by such excesses, it is prone to crumble.

In the United States before the global financial crisis, private credit grew from 143 percent of GDP in 2002 to 168 percent in 2007—a 25-percentage-point increase—and the average annual GDP growth rate slowed by two-thirds, to less than 1 percent, over the next five years.

As we know now, the US debt binge was driven in part by the rise of "subprime" lenders, many of them pushing loans on deceptively easy terms. Though only a small portion of home loans were subprime, this was a concentrated backwater of the shady private players who often appear late in a credit mania, offering loans with no money down, no proof of employment, and no debt repayment record required.

The State Follows

Typically, it is only after private lenders and borrowers get in trouble that the government gets involved. As a mania builds, authorities try to restrain the worst lending practices through regulation, but this campaign degenerates into a game of whack-a-mole. If the authorities ban subprime home loans, the credit moles start offering mobile home loans, no income required.

The party ends in many cases when the central bank is forced to raise rates to halt the credit excesses, triggering a financial crisis. The economy slows, and authorities begin working to ease the crisis by shifting the debt of bankrupt borrowers onto the government's books. Government debt rises, and rises even faster when politicians start borrowing to raise public spending in an effort to soften the economic downturn.

In a 2014 study of financial crises going back to 1870, economist Alan Taylor and his colleagues concluded, "The idea that financial crises typically have their roots in fiscal [government borrowing] problems is not supported over the long sweep of history."[4] Normally, they write, trouble begins in the private sector, though countries that enter the crisis with heavy government debt will suffer a longer and deeper recession, because the government will find it harder to borrow to finance bailouts.

The private-sector root of debt crises is well established. The IMF has identified more than 430 severe financial crises since 1970, and it classifies fewer than 70 as primarily government or "sovereign" debt crises. Those include Latin American crises of the 1980s, and the notoriety of those meltdowns helps explain why many analysts still look for a government to blame for every financial crisis.

The Record-Setting Binge in China

China's historic debt binge illustrates many classic dynamics of debt manias, but with distinctly Chinese characteristics.

When I visited Beijing in September 2008, the economy was slowing. The Shanghai stock market had just crashed. Property prices were weak. But Chinese officials were sanguine. They said China was entering the middle-income rank of nations, so it was time for it to slow down as previous Asian miracle economies, like Japan, South Korea, and Taiwan, had. They talked about cutting back on investment, downsizing large state companies, and letting the market allocate credit, which at this point was *not* growing faster than the economy. Between 2003 and 2008, credit had held steady at about 150 percent of GDP.

Two weeks after I left China, Lehman Brothers filed for bankruptcy in the United States, and global markets went into a tailspin. Demand collapsed in the United States and Europe, crushing export growth in China, where leaders panicked. By October, the government had reversed course, redoubling its commitment to the old investment-led growth model, this time by fueling the engine with debt. From 2008 through 2018, total debts would increase by $80 trillion worldwide, as countries fought off the effects of the financial crisis, but of that total, $35 trillion, or nearly half, was racked up by China alone.

By the time I returned to Beijing in August 2009, the government had launched an aggressive spending and lending program that kept China's GDP growth above 8 percent, while the United States and Europe were in recession. That steadily high GDP growth had convinced many Chinese that their government could produce any growth rate it wanted.

Bank regulators were the only officials who expressed alarm, and their main concern was increasingly reckless lending in the private sector. "Shadow banks" had started to appear, selling credit products with yields that were too high to be true. Big state banks responded with "wealth management products" that bundled their loans together with the higher-returning debts of the shadow banks. Many Chinese figured that these offerings had to be solid investments, since they were issued by big state banks. But outsiders compared them to the complex American debt products that Warren Buffett had described as "financial weapons of mass destruction"[5] before their implosion helped trigger the crisis of 2008.

By 2013, shadow banks accounted for half of the trillions of dollars in new yearly credit flows in China. The game of whack-a-mole was on. When Beijing began to limit borrowing by local governments, local authorities set up shell companies to borrow from shadow banks. Soon these "local government funding vehicles" became the biggest debtors in the shadow banking system.

As the flow of debt accelerated, more lending went to wasteful projects. By some estimates, 10 percent of the firms on the mainland stock exchange were "zombie companies," kept alive by government loans. Before 2007, it took one dollar of new debt to generate one dollar of GDP in China. Over the next five years, it took four dollars of debt to generate one dollar of GDP growth, as the state doled out loans to incompetent and failing borrowers.

Much of the lending started to flow into real estate, the worst target for investment binges. Easy loans spurred the sale of about 800 million square feet of real estate in 2010, more than in all other markets of the world combined. In big cities, prices were rising at 20 to 30 percent a year.

Caught up in the excitement, banks stopped looking at whether borrowers had income and started lending on collateral—often property. This "collateralized lending" works only as long as borrowers short on income can keep making loan payments by borrowing against the rising price of their property. By 2013, a third of the new loans in China were going to pay off old loans. That October, Bank of China chairman Xiao Gang warned that shadow banking resembled a "Ponzi scheme," with more and more loans based on "empty real estate."

At the March 2013 party congress, Li Keqiang came in as prime minister. He was one of the Chinese leaders who appeared to accept the reality that a maturing economy needed to slow down, which would allow him to restrain the credit boom. Yet every time the economy showed signs of slowing, the government would reopen the credit spigot to revive it.

The cast of dubious creditors grew increasingly flaky, including coal and steel companies with no experience in finance, guaranteeing billions of dollars in IOUs issued by their clients and partners. By 2014, lending entrepreneurs were shifting their sights from property to new markets—including the stock market.

Even the state-controlled media jumped in the game, urging ordinary Chinese to buy stocks for patriotic reasons. Their hope was to create a steady bull market and provide debt-laden state companies with a new source of funding. Instead they got one of the biggest stock bubbles in history.

There are four basic signs of a stock bubble: high levels of borrowing for stock purchases; prices rising at a pace that can't be justified by the underlying rate of economic growth; overtrading by retail investors; and exorbitant valuations. By April 2015, when the state-run *People's Daily* crowed that the good times were "just beginning," the Shanghai market had reached the extreme end of all four bubble metrics, which is rare.

The amount that Chinese investors borrowed to buy stock had set a world record, equal to 9 percent of the total value of tradable stocks. Stock prices were up 70 percent in just six months, despite slowing growth in the economy. On some days, more stock was changing hands in China than in all other stock markets combined. In June 2015 the market started to crash, and it continued to crash despite government orders to investors not to sell.

This credit binge had some characteristics unique to China's state-run system, including the borrowing by local government fronts and the Communist propaganda cheering on a capitalist bubble. But its fundamental dynamics were typical of debt manias. It began with private players, who assumed the government would not let them fail, and devolved into a game of whack-a-mole. As the government fitfully tried to contain the mania, more and more dubious lenders and borrowers got in the game, blowing bubbles in stocks and real estate. The quality of credit deteriorated sharply, into collateralized loans and IOUs. These are all important mania warning signals.

The most important sign was, as ever, private credit growing much faster than the economy. After holding steady before 2008, the debt burden exploded over the next five years, increasing by 74 percentage points as a share of GDP. This was the largest credit boom ever recorded in the emerging world (though Ireland and Spain have outdone it in the developed world).

Before China, the roster of extreme postwar credit booms included two of the earlier Asian miracles—Japan and Taiwan—as well as recent Asian Tigers such as Malaysia, Thailand, and Indonesia. None had escaped a severe economic slowdown. This did not augur well for China's chances of avoiding the kiss of debt.

By mid-2019 China had, in fact, seen economic growth slow by nearly half, from double digits to 6 percent, right in line with previous extreme binges. To date then, no country has escaped this

Ten Biggest Debt Binges

Following the biggest debt binges, GDP growth has always slowed sharply.

Country	5-Year Increase in Private Debt to GDP	Year Credit Binge Peaked	Decline in GDP Growth, Next 5 Years
Ireland	107%	2005	–5.4
Spain	90%	2005	–2.7
China	74%	2014	–2.4
UK	69%	2007	–3.7
Malaysia	68%	1995	–4.4
Thailand	67%	1993	–8.2
UK	67%	1986	–1.4
Denmark	65%	2007	–2.7
Zimbabwe	65%	2002	–7.8
Chile	64%	1982	–5.8

Source: Haver Analytics, Goldman Sachs.

rule: a five-year increase in the ratio of private credit to GDP that is more than 40 percentage points has always led to a sharp slowdown in economic growth.

China did, however, dodge the less consistent threat of a financial crisis, aided by some unexpected strengths. One was the dazzling boom in its tech sector, without which the economy would have slowed much more dramatically. Another was the fact that Chinese borrowers were in debt mainly to Chinese lenders, and in many cases the state owned both parties to the loan. In short, China was well positioned to forgive or roll over its own debts. And with strong export income, vast foreign exchange reserves, strong domestic savings, and still ample bank deposits, it had managed to avert the financial crisis that often accompanies large, debt-driven economic slowdowns.

The Shape of the Slowdown

When a credit boom goes bust, people lose faith in their future income, and in their ability to take on debts. That uncertainty leads to belt-tightening, further slowing the economy.

The path of the slowdown depends in large part on how quickly the government can stabilize the debt-to-GDP balance, either by slowing debt growth or by reviving GDP growth. In a maturing economy like China, where GDP growth is slowing naturally, the key question is how soon the government can fix the debt problem.

The other extreme credit binges offer possible scenarios. In Taiwan, as the credit crisis hit in 1992, the government responded by pulling back on lending and public investment and allowing more private banks to compete with state banks. The economy's trend growth rate did slow in the five years after the crisis, but mildly, from 9 to 7 percent, which was still solid growth for a country with per capita income around $15,000.

Another possible scenario is Japan. After its debt-fueled property and stock market bubbles collapsed in 1990, the government didn't restrain lending. It bailed out troubled borrowers, covered bad loans with new loans, and pressured banks to prop up faltering companies and fund increasingly unproductive investments, including "bridges to nowhere."

The result was rising debt and stagnant growth. Total debt rose from 250 percent of GDP in 1990 to 405 percent today. The GDP growth rate fell from nearly 5 percent before 1990 to less than 1 percent for the next quarter century. By 2019, Japan's $4 trillion economy was less than one-third as large as it would have been, had it maintained its trend growth rate of the 1980s, when it was being hyped as the next world superpower.

This is a possible future for China too, if for political reasons it attempts to prolong the life of its aging economic boom with rising debt.

The Upside: After the Bust

When massive credit binges start to unwind, and credit growth falls below the rate of economic growth, the result is often a painful recession. But that is a necessary cleansing step.

If credit has been growing slower than the economy, the banking system is most likely healing. In fact, the more slowly debt has been growing as a share of GDP over a five-year period, the more likely it is that the economy will witness an increase in growth, boosted by healthy credit, in subsequent years. Many countries have seen this kind of recovery in recent decades, including Chile after 1991, Hungary after 1995, and the Czech Republic after 2002.

Indonesia is a particularly dramatic case. Before the Asian financial crisis, the Suharto dictatorship had allowed many industrial conglomerates to establish their own banks, which came to operate as slush funds. At some banks, more than 90 percent of loans were "connected," or doled out to a parent company, subsidiaries, or top officials. By 1997, as many as 90 percent of these loans were "nonperforming"; the borrower had not made a payment in at least nine months.

Often, at the depths of a credit crisis, entrenched powers fight to hold on to the banks that they have run into insolvency. In Indonesia, the agency set up to restructure the banks started promisingly by shutting thirteen institutions owned by friends and sons of Suharto. But one son soon reemerged as head of a different bank, public confidence collapsed, and Indonesians began moving their money to foreign countries.

By early 1998 the Indonesian rupiah had lost 80 percent of its value, and banks started to unravel. State banks held about half the assets in the system, and many did not have enough deposits to back up their loans. As the extent of the rot became known, the stock market value of Indonesian banks collapsed to near zero in 1998; in the world's estimation, the Indonesian banking system had ceased to exist.

Bloody street protests broke out, forcing Suharto to resign. The bank restructuring agency began to move faster, banning many Suharto cronies from the industry for life. In a historically insular country, the new government granted foreigners the right to buy 99 percent ownership stakes in banks and to replace the old bosses with professionals.

In emerging countries, where, on average, banks still account for 80 percent of all lending (compared to 50 percent in the United States), a shake-up of banking is a shake-up of society.

To restart a banking system from zero, authorities need to recognize and dispose of bad loans, and inject new capital into banks so that they can lend again. But any action involves a political choice: who will suffer the pain? Authorities can force borrowers into default and allow lenders to seize their cars or homes. Or they can force lenders to forgive debts and ease repayment terms. Either way, the crisis begins to end not when borrowers start to repay debt, but when they are forced into default or forgiven.

Indonesia chose to punish the discredited lenders. The government took control of some $32 billion in bad bank loans, to be sold for pennies on the dollar, and forced many to merge or close. Within two years the number of banks in Indonesia had fallen from 240 to 164. Four of the worst state banks were folded into a stronger one, Bank Mandiri. Nine failed private banks were merged into Bank Danamon, whose original owner, a close Suharto associate, fled the country, owing more than $1 billion to crony banks.

Another signal that a debt crisis is bottoming out can be found on the banks' books. When banks don't hold enough deposits to cover their loans, they can face trouble, particularly if they rely on foreign funding to fill the gap. If bank loans amount to more than

100 percent of deposits, the system enters a risky zone. Past 120 percent, the system faces a crisis warning—even if the banks don't depend on foreign funding.

After the crisis hits, the ratio of loans to deposits will fall, as the bank curtails lending, writes off bad loans, and begins to attract deposits again. In general, when loans fall back under 80 percent as a share of deposits, banks will be poised to restart lending.

This return to banking-system balance has marked the revival in many postcrisis countries, including Indonesia. As crisis loomed in 1997, the average loan-to-deposit ratio hit 110 percent. After the crisis, that ratio fell to 35 percent within a year.

This drop in the loan-to-deposit ratio set the stage for a transformation. Indonesian bankers emerged from the crisis badly burned, with a sense of caution that remains today. The banks that were created from failed banks—Danamon and Mandiri—have since emerged among the best-run and most respected banks in Asia.

Debtophobia

There is a fine line, however, between healthy caution and debtophobia. After some severe crises, bankers and borrowers seem to suffer a form of posttraumatic stress. Their fear slows credit growth sharply, retarding the pace of recovery. Even in Southeast Asia, where the 1998 crisis passed quickly, it took several years for the recovery to gain momentum.

The crisis of 2008 triggered a new bout of debtophobia, and widespread fear that capitalism would grind to a halt. For many years, debt had been growing faster than the global economy, helping to spur growth. After the crisis, debt continued to grow rapidly only in China and a handful of other countries, while it slowed in the rest of the world. Many nations succumbed at least for a time to debtophobia, including the United States, where debt growth plummeted as households started to retrench and their savings rates went up.

Researchers assessing this shift found many historical cases in which economies began to grow again after a crisis, even if debtophobia reigned and credit remained stagnant. The catch is that these "creditless recoveries" tend to be very weak, with GDP growth rates around one-third lower than in a credit-fueled recovery.[6]

Mexico knows this pain well. After the 1994 crisis destroyed Mexican banks, their owners managed to delay any cleanup of bad loans, and the banks lacked the deposits to make new loans. Mexicans came to distrust bankers, and to this day many don't keep a bank account. Between 1994 and 2018, Mexico saw private bank credit shrink as a share of GDP from 38 to 20 percent, and growth stagnated. During this period, neighbors like Chile and Brazil surpassed Mexico in terms of average per capita income.

Mexico's debtophobia has now lasted nearly as long as the case suffered by the United States after the crash of 1929. For the next twenty-five years, as British economist Tim Congdon has argued, Americans' traditional optimism gave way to doubt, marked by "extreme caution" toward new lending.[7]

Normally, debtophobia is less persistent. Looking at financial crises back to the 1930s, Empirical Research, a New York–based consulting firm, found that on average, credit and economic growth remained weak for about four to five years.[8] In Asia, credit fell in the five years after 1997 by at least 40 percentage points as a share of GDP in Indonesia, Thailand, and Malaysia. But within about four years, the gloom had started to lift as debts fell, government deficits declined, and global prices for the region's commodity exports rose. Credit growth picked up, and the average GDP growth rate in these three Southeast Asian economies rose from around 4 percent between 1999 and 2002 to nearly 6 percent between 2003 and 2006.*

Thus, the upside of the credit rule is that five-year runs of weak credit growth often lead to a stronger run of economic growth.

How Paying Off Debt Pays Off

Before 2000, many emerging countries had never seen a period of real financial stability, or a healthy credit boom. Inflation was high and volatile, and when prices for big-ticket items are unpredictable, banks won't dare make loans that extend for more than a few months. In emerging countries, many cornerstones of American consumer culture and middle-class existence, including the five-year car loan and the thirty-year mortgage, had been unimaginable luxuries.

Then the new generation of emerging-world leaders began controlling deficits and lowering inflation, and this newly stable environment quickly led to a revolution in lending. Credit cards and corporate bonds were introduced for the first time. Mortgages, which barely existed in 2000, became a multibillion-dollar industry,

---

* South Korea, another country at the center of the Asian financial crisis, is excluded here because it followed a different pattern and never saw a decline in credit growth.

rising from 0 percent of GDP to 7 percent in Brazil and Turkey, 4 percent in Russia, and 3 percent in Indonesia by 2013. For countries where people cannot buy a car or a house unless they amass enough cash, the introduction of these simple credit products is as important a step into the modern world as indoor plumbing.

Periods of healthy credit growth bear no psychological resemblance to the extreme exuberance of manias or the extreme caution of debtophobia. In place of shady lenders and unqualified borrowers, responsible lenders are widening the choice of solid loan options, creating a more balanced economy. When the global financial crisis hit in 2008, countries like the United States were vulnerable because they had been running up debt too fast. In Southeast Asia, however, the opposite story was unfolding.

Indonesia, Thailand, Malaysia, and the Philippines had manageable debt burdens and strong banks ready to lend, with total loans less than 80 percent of deposits. Over the next five years the health of the credit system would prove crucial: nations such as Spain and Greece, which had seen the sharpest increase in debt before 2008, would post the slowest growth after the crisis; nations such as the Philippines and Thailand, which had seen the smallest increase in debt during the boom, would fare the best.

This is how the credit cycle works in brief: Rising debt can be a sign of healthy growth, unless debt is growing much faster than the economy for too long. The size of the debt matters, but the pace of increase is the most important sign of change for the better or the worse. The first signs of trouble often appear in the private sector, where credit manias tend to originate.

The psychology of a debt binge encourages lending mistakes and borrowing excesses that will retard growth and possibly lead to a financial crisis. The crisis can inspire a healthy new caution, or a paralyzing fear of debt. Either way, the period of retrenchment usually lasts only a few years. The country emerges with lower debts, bankers ready to lend, and an economy poised to grow rapidly.

10

HYPE

Successful Nations Rise outside the Spotlight

For most of my career I have worked as a writer and an investor, and I have come to see how differently Fleet Street and Wall Street view time. The nature of their jobs requires investors to train their eyes on the future; journalists, on the present. Market players make money by being early to the next big trend, but the media consider a trend credible only after it has been running for a few years. They are often slower to see big shifts in the story.

A classic case is the rise and fall of hype for Japan. Even after Tokyo markets crashed in 1990, the global media and political elite kept talking up Japan as the superpower of the future. In early 1992, *Time* magazine ran a cover touting predictions that Japan could overtake the United States as the world's largest economy within a decade. In the US presidential race that year, candidate Paul Tsongas declared: "The Cold War is over and Japan has won."[1]

By 1994, Japan was deep in a slump and the media had dumped it for the "Asian Tigers"—particularly Thailand, Indonesia, and Malaysia. Countless articles linked their success to the "Asian values" of thriftiness and hard work, right up until the crisis of 1997, which exposed their taste for luxury goods and dollar debt.

Then the mood shifted from love to hate, as it often does. The media began churning out exposés on Asian "crony capitalism," the corrupt fortune amassed by Indonesian leader Suharto, and so on. By 2003, if the press mentioned the Asian economies, it was dismissively, as in a *Time* cover that year titled "Tigers No More." Over the next five years, as if to prove the media wrong, Southeast Asia took off amid a broad boom in emerging economies.

The longer an economic boom or bust lasts, the more likely it is to end, but the media become more and more convinced it will never end. Instead of recognizing the cyclical nature of economic trends, they assume that long booms will become more deeply entrenched and stable over time. Their admiring coverage, in turn, makes national leaders too complacent to keep pushing reform, and hastens the inevitable crisis.

When a crisis hits and media love turns to hate, the criticism is often well founded: the stew of crony capitalist practices exposed during the Asian financial crisis was very real. But a turnaround is still far off. Messes take time to fix.

The next economic stars often emerge from among countries that have fallen off the media radar, after the crisis has passed. They start to recover momentum when left alone to put their economic house in order, and it is only after they record several years of strong growth that the media rediscover them. By then, the run may be nearing exhaustion.

The reality is that successful nations often rise from the shadows, and those getting the most hype are often the most likely to stumble in coming years. Media love is a bad sign, and media indifference is a good one.

A Brief History of Emerging-World Hype

In the early twentieth century, the few people who paid attention to global economic competition were focused on Latin America and particularly Argentina, which had attained first-world income levels by taking advantage of a new British invention—the refrigerated steamship—to export its beef and crops. Argentina was one of the world's richest economies in the 1950s, but it was failing to modernize under the populist misrule of Juan Perón, and the hype was shifting to Venezuela, which tapped its vast petroleum reserves to prosper as oil prices spiked in the 1970s. Venezuela reached an income level close to that of the United States in that decade and was touted as a rising capitalist democracy on a continent where dictators were taking over.

Pundits of the 1950s and '60s largely ignored Asia, and when they hyped any Asian country, they focused on the Philippines and Burma, both rich in natural resources. They pitied China and India as hopelessly mired in poverty, and dismissed Taiwan as a "basket case" with a corrupt government presiding over a largely illiterate population.[2] They saw South Korea as a "rat hole" into which Washington was dumping aid dollars with no visible effect.[3]

These predictions were wrong for both continents and countries. Since the 1970s, Asia's average income has been catching up to the West, but Latin America has fallen behind. Argentina continued to tread water, and Venezuela fell back as oil prices retreated in the 1980s. Within Asia, Burma faltered even before the 1962 coup turned it into a failed military state. Burma was followed down the tubes by the Phillipines, under the Marcos regime. Meanwhile, Taiwan the "basket case" and South Korea the "rat hole" were on the rise. In the 1980s and '90s, when China and then India began their transformations, they also took off outside the global media spotlight.

The Cover Curse

The backward-looking nature of journalism is captured in an old joke: By the time a story reaches the cover of *Time* or *Newsweek*, it's dead.

To test that proposition, I reviewed *Time* covers published between 1980 and 2010 and found 122 featuring an economic take on a country or region. (*Newsweek* got a pass for lack of access to its archives.) If the *Time* cover was downbeat, economic growth picked up over the next five years in 55 percent of the cases. In March 1982, *Time* invoked "Interest Rate Anguish" over US Fed chair Paul Volcker's decision to hike interest rates—a move now widely lauded for ending a period of stagflation. In August 1999, *Time*'s cover "Japan Returns to Nationalism" saw the country turning inward, but Japan began to push reform and pick up some speed.

On the other hand, if *Time*'s cover was upbeat, the economy slowed down over the next five years in 66 percent of the cases. This happened thirty-seven times between 1980 and 2010. The May 2006 cover extolling "The French Way of Reform" was followed by a five-year fall in the growth rate. *Time* would ask whether this is "China's Century—or India's?" in November 2011, the year when the big emerging economies started to slow dramatically.

There are exceptions, such as the *Economist*, perhaps thanks to its deliberately contrarian worldview. On the basis of 209 covers between 1980 and 2010 when the *Economist*'s take was optimistic, the economy improved over the next five years in roughly two-thirds of the cases. When the *Economist*'s take was gloomy, the economy slowed more than half the time.

The Limits of Linear Thinking

The point here is not to pick on weekly newsmagazines, which are, in any event, a dying breed in the internet age. It is to highlight the problem of linear thinking, which is alive and well in journalism.

Reporters tend to follow the lead of authorities like the IMF, which show a systematic tendency to hype hot economies. In 2013, former US Treasury secretary Larry Summers and Lant Pritchett issued a paper that pleaded with forecasters to recognize overwhelming research showing that economies tend to "regress to the mean"—in other words, fall to the historic mean GDP growth rate for all countries. (That mean rate is about 3.5 percent, or 1.8 percent for per capita income growth.)

By assuming, in a linear way, that India and China would continue to grow at roughly their current pace, the IMF forecasts had these two economies quadrupling in size by 2030, for a combined expansion of about $53 trillion. If India and China instead saw growth regress to the mean, Summers and Pritchett wrote, they would only double in size by 2030, for a combined expansion of $11 trillion. That's a $42 trillion gap.[4] It is this kind of straight-line forecast that induces "Asiaphoria"—a tendency to hype Asian economies.

Economists tend to change forecasts in small increments and miss big shifts. By early 2008 there were warning signs, including a fall in the stock market, that the Great Recession had already begun. But none of the fifty leading forecasters who are surveyed quarterly by the Philadelphia branch of the Fed saw it coming. Their average forecast dropped a bit, but only two of the fifty predicted growth below 1 percent for 2008, and not one predicted negative growth. We now know that the Great Recession had started in 2007.

Similarly, in a study of IMF forecasts for 189 countries between 1999 and 2014, the *Economist* found 220 cases in which an economy grew one year but shrank the next. In its April forecasts for the coming year, however, the IMF never once saw the contraction coming. Though economics was derided by historian Thomas Carlyle as the "dismal science," it is often prone to "optimism bias."

I suspect the IMF and the World Bank are reluctant to offend high officials in countries that are also their clients—hence their optimism bias. But independent analysts face similar pressures. Economists covering China have complained to me that if they question government growth claims, they will get an earful from Beijing; but if they don't, they will hear it from skeptical investors.

Group Think, Group Hype

After 2002, the combination of easy money, rising trade, and high commodity prices triggered an unprecedented boom. Over the next five years, the 150 emerging countries tracked by the IMF saw growth more than double, to an average rate of more than 7 percent. Forecasters projected that large emerging economies, including Brazil, Russia, India, and China, would continue to expand at a torrid pace, and that their average incomes would eventually catch up with those of the developed world.

Thus was born the myth of "mass convergence," a worldwide leveling of incomes. This scenario had a beguiling appeal to many people, from NGOs rooting for the poor to global investors hoping to make a fortune in emerging markets. It seemed plausible at the time. Between 2005 and 2010, 107 of the 110 emerging countries in the authoritative Penn Table database were gaining on the United States in terms of average income. The three countries losing ground were Niger, Eritrea, and Jamaica—small exceptions that appeared to prove the rule of mass convergence.

The convergence boom, however, was freakishly unusual. In every decade between 1960 and 2000, the per capita income of most emerging nations fell relative to the United States. When the boom began after the turn of the millennium, the narrative shifted and the mass convergence story took hold, implying that most developing nations were on track to reach the developed class. The optimism didn't last long.

In 2010, growth started to slow in the emerging world as global capital flows and trade ebbed, and commodity prices weakened. By

The Myth of Mass Convergence

Before 2000, most emerging countries were falling behind the United States in average income—or deconverging—most of the time.

	Number of Emerging-Market Countries	Number of EM Countries Deconverging	Deconvergence Rate
1950s	37	15	40.5%
1960s	77	46	59.7%
1970s	95	51	53.7%
1980s	97	75	77.3%
1990s	120	83	69.2%
2000s	112	12	10.7%
2010-18	111	28	25.2%

Source: World Bank, Haver Analytics.

mid-decade, the average growth rate in emerging nations had fallen from the 2010 peak of 7.5 percent to its long-term average of 4 percent, and to around 2 percent excluding China. The United States was growing faster than the average for emerging economies. Far from converging, many of the most hyped emerging economies, including Russia, Brazil, and South Africa, were falling behind the United States.

The Special Problem of Hype for Commodity Economies

Blanket hype for emerging markets makes no distinction between manufacturing economies that grow by making things, such as China, and commodity economies that grow by pumping stuff out of the ground, like Brazil. This distinction makes a huge difference. Most emerging economies are driven by commodity exports and tend to rise and fall with global prices for those exports.

In the 1970s, when a standard index of commodity prices rose 160 percent, 28 nations saw their average income converge rapidly with incomes in the West.* But when commodity prices stagnated in the 1980s and '90s, the number of rapidly converging nations fell to 11; as commodity prices doubled after 2000, the number bounced back up to 37.

The erratic path of commodity economies was demonstrated in stark relief by a commission that the World Bank assembled in 2008, under Nobel laureate Michael Spence, to unravel the secrets of long, steady growth booms that had appeared only in the post-war era. The Spence Commission identified thirteen economies that had posted average growth of more than 7 percent over at least a quarter century, but these stories had very different endings.[5] Only six reached a high income level, and five of those six were export-manufacturing powers, with the quirky exception of Malta. Of the seven economies that stalled before reaching a high income level, six were commodity-rich: Botswana, Indonesia, Malaysia, Oman, Thailand, and Brazil. Rising and falling with prices for iron ore and soybeans, Brazil's per capita income is just 16 percent of per capita income in the United States, basically the same as it was in 1914.

Raw materials often play an outsize role in shaping an economy's future. Income from natural resources accounts for 8 percent of GDP, on average, in low- and middle-income countries, compared to 1.4 percent in developed countries. This 8 percent share may sound small, but it can determine an economy's fate if it accounts

---

* "Rapid convergence" defined: I looked at growth in 173 nations going back to 1960 and then ranked these nations by how much their per capita GDP rose compared to per capita GDP in the United States, in each decade. The top quarter of all these observations were designated as "rapid convergence" cases. In these cases, per capita GDP rose by at least 2.8 percentage points, as a share of US per capita GDP, over the decade.

for a significant portion of exports or government revenues. Rapid commodity price shifts can suddenly pinch revenues and trigger a crisis—particularly if the country needs foreign revenue to service foreign debts. Oil accounts for only 10 percent of Russian GDP, but also for half of exports and a third of government revenue, making the economy hugely vulnerable to oil prices.

In 2014, several magazines feted President Putin as "the most powerful man in the world" following the Russian invasion of Crimea.[6] But that same year oil prices collapsed, cutting the average Russian income by a third. This was a classic case of hype peaking at the end of a trend.

The Rosy Disaster Scenarios

One of the stranger forms of hype is the Malthusian disaster scenario, inspired by early-nineteenth-century English scholar Thomas Malthus. Ever since Malthus predicted that population growth would outpace farm output, experts have been periodically echoing his warning. They forecast that rising food prices will bring famine to huge swaths of the world, and potentially huge fortunes to farm regions.

But Malthusians make the same mistake that Malthus made: they underestimate how quickly farmers respond to prices. As prices rise, farmers invest some of the profit to increase production, thus keeping prices down and ensuring that people can afford food. In fact, studies show that farmers respond faster to market forces than do other big commodity suppliers, such as multinational oil companies.

Since World War II, global food prices adjusted for inflation have fallen at an average annual pace of 1.7 percent. In many countries, there is room to boost supply further. Crop yields are about half as high in China, Brazil, and the former Soviet countries as they are in the United States, so output could rise radically if these countries copy foreign methods.

In 2011, Malthusians were on red alert. Prices had surged 66 percent in the previous two years, and Oxfam was warning that inflation would drive millions more people into hunger by 2030. Between 2000 and 2010, however, the world had invested $1 trillion in the production of raw materials, including soybeans and other foods. As production rose, food prices fell 30 percent between 2011 and 2013. The Malthusian pessimism about famine—and optimism about food exporters like Brazil—vanished, at least for the time being.

The Income Traps

One reason to be wary about hype for the future of hot economies is the harsh reality of income traps, which can spring on countries at every step of the development ladder.

The conventional view is that there is one trap, which trips up economies when they reach the middle-income level. A poor nation can grow rapidly by making simple improvements, such as paving roads and moving farmers into more productive factory jobs. But it becomes much more difficult to sustain growth when the country reaches the middle-income level and it needs to develop more advanced industries.

The middle-income trap is real, but it is not the only one. The challenges of generating sustainable growth and productive industry—underpinned by solid institutions and steady infusions of investment and credit—do not accumulate and confront an economy all at once. They hound nations that are extremely rich, extremely poor, and everything in between.

World Bank researchers coined the phrase "middle-income trap" in 2007, but in 2013 a different team at the bank found "very little" evidence that the trap exists.[7] Economies get bogged down at all income levels, not just the middle. The researchers cited countries, like Bangladesh, that had stalled at a very low income; and others, like Japan, Ireland, and the United Kingdom, that had suffered prolonged slowdowns when they were quite rich.

In any decade, more nations on average fall back to a lower income level than advance to a higher one. Since the late 1940s, many nations have experienced this downward mobility, including the Philippines in the 1950s and Russia, South Africa, and Iran in the 1980s and '90s.

Development traps can drag newly rich countries back to the middle-income ranks, as has happened at least three times in the last century. Venezuela made the round trip from middle class to rich and back within the last 100 years. Argentina's average income fell from 65 percent of the US level in the 1930s to less than 20 percent by 2010. Most recently, Greece was demoted from developed to emerging-market status after its financial crisis in 2010.

It's also common to fall back into poverty. In a 2012 study, the World Bank identified 13 emerging countries that, over the last half century, managed to rise from the poor or middle class into the high-income class, and they include the famous Asian "miracles." But the same study identified a much larger group of countries, 31, that, over the same period, fell from middle income to low income, including Iraq, Afghanistan, and Haiti.

The way economists put it is that strong growth shows little "persistence." Summers and Pritchett analyzed all twenty-eight nations that, since 1950, have experienced periods of "super rapid growth," defined as an average annual per capita GDP growth rate of 6 percent for at least eight years. They found that these booms tend to be "extremely short lived," dying out after a median duration of nine years, and "nearly always" ending in a significant slowdown. Typically, the economy returned to per capita growth of just over 2 percent, a rate that is "near complete regression to the mean" for all nations.[8] That's worth keeping in mind, when reading stories touting countries in the midst of long booms as the economies of the future.

Why the Opposite of Love Is Indifference

The fastest-growing economies are almost always found among the poorer nations, because it is easier to grow rapidly from a low income base. And these rising economies also tend to be ignored by the global media until they have been booming for many years.

In the decades between 1950 and 2010, per capita income in the ten fastest-growing economies was, on average, less than $3,000 at the start of their hot decade. Those cases include Nigeria and Israel during the 1960s, Indonesia and Mexico during the 1970s, Korea and China during the 1980s, Poland and China again in the 1990s.

Today's developed countries rarely made the list, outside the post-war recovery decade of the 1950s, when Germany, Japan, and Italy were all in the top ten.

The rate of churn on my top ten lists* has been remarkable. Three of the ten fastest growing economies from the 1950s repeated the feat in the '60s, but none from the 1960s repeated in the '70s. Only one from the 1970s, South Korea, returned to the top ten list in the '80s. Just two from the 1980s—South Korea and China—made the top ten in the '90s. And one from the '90s, China, returned the following decade. In addition, many countries have hit the top ten for one decade and never appeared again, including Jamaica, Bulgaria, Hungary, Mexico, Cameroon, Angola, and Kazakhstan.

When booms go bust, the media conduct an autopsy, laying bare all the spending and debt excesses racked up in the late stages of the boom. The government sets up commissions to close banks and dispose of bad loans, replace corrupt and incompetent figures at leading state companies, and push reform designed to make sure the same crisis doesn't recur.

The housecleaning can take several years, so expecting a fast turnaround can be costly. Acting on the advice of Baron de Rothschild, who said the best time to buy is when there is "blood in the streets," many global investors bought into Thailand in the summer of 1997, only to see Thai stocks fall another 70 percent.

Economies are most likely to turn for the better not during the period of hate but after the media have moved on. By the year 2000,

---

* See the appendix for my list of the top ten fastest-growing economies by decade, back to 1950.

the global media had turned its back on Thailand and emerging markets in general. It was during this period that new leaders in Russia, Turkey, South Korea, and Brazil began working out of the limelight on the dull reforms—bringing current accounts back into balance and debts under control—that would set the stage for the next emerging-world boom.

Economic growth lacks persistence, but media negativity often shows tremendous persistence. The Philippines, for example, had been an Imelda Marcos joke for so long that few journalists took seriously its revival under President Benigno "Noynoy" Aquino, who took power in 2010. Under him, the Philippines became the world's fastest-growing economy, but journalist friends continued to laugh when I touted its prospects. Straight-line pessimism is as misleading as straight-line optimism.

In any five-year economic cycle, the competitive landscape can change completely. As some nations reach the peak of a debt binge, others will be busy paying off debts, setting themselves up for strong growth. Even commodity countries are poised to boom like a clock every time commodity prices begin an upward swing. In September 1998, *Time* put the crisis-wracked Russian economy on a cover that said "Help!" but over the next five years Russia's growth accelerated from negative 5 percent to positive 7 percent, as oil prices rose — and the government began wisely saving the profits for a rainy day.

The hype rule comes down to a few simple observations: Wise national leaders try not to let hype go to their heads and keep pushing reform even when the economy is roaring and the world is applauding. Good forecasters know to look for the next big success stories not among the nations most loved or hated by the markets and media, but among the forgotten and ignored. As the writer and Holocaust survivor Elie Wiesel has said, the opposite of love is not hate; it is indifference.[9]

Ten Rules, One Goal

Mainstream opinion typically gets the future wrong, because it extrapolates recent trends in a straight line and grows more enamored of a country the longer its growth run lasts. The way to avoid falling for the hype is to monitor the ten rules outlined in this book.

Rarely will any country look good on all ten. But together, the rules sketch the ideal habits of successful nations. First, nations in this elite class battle the global slowdown in working-age population growth by recruiting women, immigrants, the elderly, and even robots into the labor force. If the labor force is stagnating or shrinking, the economy probably will be too.

Successful nations have a strong sense of urgency, often inspired by a recent crisis, and they choose political leaders who are willing to push tough economic reform. Ideally, they are democracies and pick their leaders in fair elections: autocrats can force rapid growth, but it tends to be erratic, and prone to collapse.

Leaders of successful nations tend to be politicians with a broad following who can rally public support for reform. They listen to experts, but are rarely technocrats themselves, and are usually new to office. Even great reformers grow stale with time.

Successful nations build governments that are right-sized: neither bloated and smothering, nor too small to provide the basics of commercial life—police, schools, roads, telephone networks. Their government spending is not excessively high or low, compared to other nations in their income class.

Led by their private entrepreneurs, successful nations invest at a healthy rate, roughly in the range of 25 to 35 percent of GDP. Investment spending is more volatile than spending by government or consumers, and a much better predictor of economic booms and busts—but it matters where the money is going. Investment binges in real estate and commodities tend to fuel empty bubbles; booms in technology and manufacturing tend to leave behind productive assets, even after they go bust.

Successful nations tend to have a healthy balance of wealth, even at the top. The total wealth of their billionaires is generally neither too far above the average for large countries (10 percent of GDP) nor too far below. Healthy economies should generate billionaires, preferably good billionaires in productive and widely popular industries such as consumer goods. If billionaire wealth is concentrating in the hands of tycoons who inherited their wealth, or who made fortunes in unproductive and corruption-prone industries like real estate and commodities, it can provoke populist revolts against the process of wealth creation itself.

Successful nations also make the most of their geographic location, investing heavily in roads, ports, and communication networks to connect themselves to global and regional markets. Rather than hoarding wealth and power, the nation's capital works to ensure that these investments bring its second cities into the global commercial mainstream. Again, balance is key. The luckier ones are already located on existing global trade routes, where export manufacturing and global service hubs are most likely to flourish.

The investment habits of successful nations help contain inflation, by building supply networks that can meet demand when the economy accelerates. As a result, their inflation rates rarely exceed the current averages of 2 percent for developed and 4 percent for emerging economies. More important, their central banks manage the supply of credit with an eye to inflation in financial markets, as well as in consumer prices. Increasingly, modern recessions follow from bubbles in stocks, bonds, and other financial assets.

Paradoxically, successful nations feel cheap, particularly to foreigners. Their currencies are inexpensive, making local prices attractive to international tourists and investors. The best test is how cheap a cup of coffee or other local goods "feel" to outsiders, because the technical measures of currency value are flawed. Cheap is good, unless the currency is also unstable, which can trigger a financial crisis.

Crisis warnings start to ring if the country has been borrowing heavily abroad to live beyond its means, a habit that will generate a steady increase in the current account deficit. My research shows that today, if the current account deficit has been above 3 percent of GDP for five years running, the nation faces a serious risk of crisis. To anticipate such crises, follow the locals; in most currency crises, locals and not big global investors are the first to spot signs of trouble, and to start moving money abroad.

Successful nations insulate themselves from these crises in two ways. First, they borrow abroad to buy factory equipment rather than consumer goods, which is investing in future growth, not living beyond their means. If investment is strong, a current account deficit is much less alarming. Second, they do not manipulate the price of the currency—a habit that in today's alert global markets only provokes rival nations to retaliate in kind.

They also avoid both debt mania, and debtophobia. A mania is brewing when debts are growing significantly faster than the economy, for an extended period. The level of debt as a share of GDP matters, but the pace of increase matters more. Typically, manias start in the private sector, and public debt rises later, as the government steps in to rescue private debtors, and starts borrowing to stimulate the floundering economy.

My research shows that if private debt increases by more than 40 percentage points as a share of GDP over five years, an economic downturn has always followed. Typically, the downturn was severe, and in three out of every five cases it was accompanied by a financial crisis. Afterward, caution often reigns, and a long period of falling debts puts the nation in position to start borrowing—and growing—again. Following severe crises, however, caution can devolve into fear. Debtophobia paralyzes the economy, and hampers recovery for many years.

Often, quietly reforming nations fall off the radar of the global markets and media, which is right where they want to be. The most loved nations rarely have the best economic prospects in the next five to ten years. The most hated nations, on the other hand, are often under fire for good reason, after a crisis has exposed flaws that will take time to fix. It is after these crisis-struck nations fade from the media glare that they are most likely to emerge as economic success stories.

An obvious question, though, is, How do we define success? That definition has changed dramatically since the global financial crisis, owing to the four Ds: depopulation as labor forces shrink, declining productivity, the deglobalization of trade and capital flows, and a global debt burden that is now at a record 320 percent of global GDP.

As a result, global growth has slowed from 4 percent, its average annual pace from 1950 through 2008, to less than 3 percent. Given the staying power of the four Ds, there is little prospect of a return to pre-2008 growth rates in the foreseeable future. This is a major downshift, and it means that every class of countries needs to reset its economic ambitions at a lower, more realistic level. The benchmark definition of rapid growth should come down from 3 percent to between 1 and 2 percent for developed countries; from 5 percent to between 3 and 4 percent for middle-income countries such as China; and from 7 to 5 percent for emerging countries such as India.

Remember, too, that the longer a growth spurt lasts, the less likely it is to continue, which is why I constantly update where countries rank on the rules and limit forecasts to five years. To those who thirst for longer-range forecasts, it is worth recalling that very few countries ever rise steadily for many decades, and those precious few generally stay within the sweet spots and out of the red zones outlined in the rules, one year at a time.

That was the case with the East Asian "miracles": they grew for decades because, for the most part, they stayed within the boundaries set by the rules. They kept pushing reform and grew in a balanced way, without serious violations of the rules on leadership, inequality, investment, inflation, credit, currency, or hype. They chose serious reformers over charming demagogues, generated billionaires mostly of the good kind, invested more in factories than frivolities, kept inflation and debts in check, avoided manic run-ups in their currencies, and didn't fall for their own hype or lose their zest for reform.

Eventually, even miracles fade, however. Every nation will go through periods of expansion and decline, and none are destined to rise, or fall, forever. In an impermanent world, the only constant is the turning of the economic and political cycles that govern the future.

ACKNOWLEDGMENTS

For the first two decades of my alternative career as a writer, I was resigned to author Christopher Hitchens's advice: "Everybody does have a book in them, but in most cases that's where it should stay." I was comfortable writing op-eds, but the thought of writing a book seemed much too daunting. All that changed thanks to Tony Emerson, who left his job as the editor of *Newsweek International* in 2010 to help me pen *Breakout Nations*. He has since become my partner for all my writing ventures. Once the book-writing bug gets you, there is no letting the ideas stay inside. *The 10 Rules of Successful Nations*, abridged and adapted from *The Rise and Fall of Nations* (W. W. Norton, 2016), is my latest project made possible with Tony's help.

I am fortunate to have one of the best research teams in the business, led by Jitania Kandhari. I have interacted with Jitania since 1998 and can only marvel at her boundless energy and enthusiasm for economic research. I am eternally grateful to her for being there for me whenever I have needed any guidance or assistance. I'd also like to thank Steven Quattry, an anchor of the team who may be the most well-read person I have ever met. His interests go well beyond the field of economics and politics, and his lateral thinking has contributed significantly to my understanding of the world. I would also like to extend my gratitude to former team members Soham Sengupta for his rigorous research on *Rise and Fall*, and Karen Leiton for her extensive work updating that research for *10 Rules*. It is hard to imagine, though, how I could get anything done without Paul Weiner. He has been the team's quartermaster and more for over a dozen years and has been involved in all my endeavors. Quick-thinking Christine Dsouza plays a similar role in Mumbai.

Ever since I started writing in 1991, my sister, Shumita Deveshwar, has been there to constantly support me, from storing relevant newspaper clippings to reviewing all my pieces. Before Tony arrived on the scene, Shumita would drop everything to edit my articles. I can't possibly repay the unconditional support I have received from her and from my parents, who have indulged my idiosyncrasies from the get-go.

My close friend and mentor Simran Bhargava has probably had the biggest influence on my thinking and writings over the years. She taught me how, in Rudyard Kipling's words, to keep your head when all about you are losing theirs, and instilled in me the basic lesson that if you can't explain something simply, you haven't understood it well enough.

There are few acts as selfless as reading someone else's book line by line and offering detailed feedback. I have been incredibly fortunate to find many people who spent long hours offering invaluable insights on the original *Rise and Fall* manuscript. Sincere thanks to Dorab Sopariwala, one of India's most respected researchers; to writer and editor Rahul Sharma; to my friend Sabah Ashraf; to Pierre Yared of Columbia University; and to my colleagues Ashutosh Sinha, Paul Psaila, Jim Upton, Swanand Kelkar, and Amay Hattangadi.

I would like to thank colleague Amy Oldenburg for all her support in my writing endeavors, and to many colleagues who made significant contributions on specific chapters and topics: Tim Drinkall, Eric Carlson, Cristina Piedrahita, Gaite Ali, Pierre Horvilleur, Vishal Gupta, Jorge Chirino, Samuel Rhee, Munib Madni, May Yu, and Gary Cheung. Cyril Moulle-Berteaux has long been my intellectual sparring partner, and I brainstormed with him on many ideas for this book. He has the best analytical mind of anyone I know.

I am also lucky to work with two of the sharpest editors in publishing, and would like to thank Stuart Proffitt at Allen Lane and Brendan Curry at Norton for the time they take promoting my projects and streamlining my prose. I am also obliged to my agent, the legendary Andrew Wylie, and his London associate James Pullen, for supporting this venture.

As both an investor and a writer, I am fortunate to have access to top-notch research firms and analysts across the world. While I can't list everyone I spoke to in connection with this book, I would like to particularly thank Dan Fineman.

Fareed Zakaria is an inspiration to many people involved with current affairs, and I have been lucky enough to have him as a close friend. He has often emphasized to me the role that writing books plays in "deepening one's intellectual capital," and his constant encouragement has been vital for me to put pen to paper.

When I look back at all the people who have helped me in writing *Rise and Fall*, and refining it in the *10 Rules*, I am struck by the generosity of so many people. While grateful to all of them, I am reminded of the story of two politicians who graduated from the same college: At their reunion, the first signed the yearbook, "I am who I am because of this college." To which the second wrote, "Why blame the college?" Similarly, the people acknowledged here are not to blame if my book does not appeal to you in the end.

APPENDIX

The Fifty-Six Postwar Success Stories

This is the list used for my studies of the impact of population, inflation, investment, and commodities on GDP growth. It uses a ten-year rolling window to smooth our yearly noise in real GDP growth, and data for the years between 1960 and 2010.

	Country	Period	Real GDP (Average Growth)		Country	Period	Real GDP (Average Growth)
1	Algeria	1963–1981	7.5	16	Hong Kong	1961–1995	8.4
2	Angola	1994–2010	9.5	17	Hungary	1966–1975	6.3
3	Azerbaijan	1995–2010	7.2	18	India	1994–2010	7.1
4	Bahrain	1998–2008	6	19	Indonesia	1964–1997	6.6
5	Belarus	1996–2010	7.1	20	Iran	1966–1978	8.9
6	Brazil	1961–1981	6.8	21	Ireland	1989–2007	6.1
7	Cameroon	1969–1987	7	22	Israel	1961–1978	7.4
8	Chile	1984–2001	6.3	23	Japan	1961–1977	7.6
9	China	1962–2010	9	24	Kenya	1961–1981	6.3
10	Costa Rica	1961–1979	6.2	25	Korea	1961–2000	7.8
11	Dominican Republic	1961–1981	6.6	26	Lebanon	1976–1987	6.2
				27	Malaysia	1961–1985	6.8
12	Ecuador	1964–1981	6	28	Mexico	1961–1982	6.5
13	Egypt	1968–1986	6.1	29	Morocco	1967–1977	6.8
14	Estonia	1995–2008	6.3	30	Myanmar	1990–2010	8.5
15	Guatemala	1968–1977	6.2	31	Nigeria	1997–2010	6.3

	Country	Period	Real GDP (Average Growth)
32	Oman	1961–1993	11.8
33	Pakistan	1961–1973	6.2
34	Panama	1961–1975	6.9
35	Paraguay	1967–1985	6.2
36	Portugal	1961–1974	6.7
37	Qatar	1991–2010	10.4
38	Romania	1971–1984	7.8
39	Russia	1999–2008	6.9
40	Saudi Arabia	1969–1982	10.6
41	Singapore	1961–2002	8.2
42	Spain	1961–1974	7.2
43	Sudan	1996–2010	6.4
44	Syria	1961–1984	7

	Country	Period	Real GDP (Average Growth)
45	Taiwan	1961–2000	8.4
46	Tanzania	1998–2010	6.3
47	Thailand	1961–1998	7
48	Tunisia	1963–1981	6.5
49	Turkey	1963–1973	5.8
50	Turkmenistan	1995–2010	9.3
51	Uganda	1987–2010	6.8
52	Ukraine	1999–2008	6.2
53	United Arab Emirates	1971–1985	12
54	Uzbekistan	1999–2010	6.5
55	Vietnam	1984–2010	6.9
56	Yemen	1971–1985	7.4

The Fastest Countries

These are lists of the top ten fastest-growing economies
in each decade going back to the 1950s, cited in chapter 10.

		In US Dollars	
Growth Ranking	1950s	1950s Real GDP per Capita CAGR*	Nominal GDP per Capita** in 1950
1	Iraq	7.9%	—
2	Libya	7.9%	—
3	Germany	7.7%	—
4	Japan	7.5%	—
5	Jamaica	7.0%	—
6	Italy	6.7%	—
7	Austria	6.4%	—
8	Bulgaria	5.8%	—
9	Guinea-Bissau	5.6%	—
10	Greece	5.5%	—
Growth Ranking	1960s	1960s Real GDP per Capita CAGR*	Nominal GDP per Capita** in 1960
1	Libya	17.4%	—
2	Oman	15.1%	—
3	Japan	9.5%	479
4	Nigeria	7.6%	93
5	Cyprus	7.4%	—
6	Montenegro	7.1%	—
7	Greece	7.1%	534
8	Hong Kong	7.0%	429
9	Israel	6.8%	1,229
10	Iran	6.8%	192
	Average		493
Growth Ranking	1970s	1970s Real GDP per Capita CAGR*	Nominal GDP per Capita** in 1970
1	Malta	8.7%	828
2	Korea	8.2%	279
3	Iraq	7.9%	331

4	Norway	7.4%	3,306
5	Gabon	7.3%	549
6	Malaysia	6.8%	358
7	Indonesia	6.6%	80
8	Algeria	6.3%	336
9	Mexico	6.1%	690
10	Congo, Repub. of	5.8%	207
	Average		**696**
Growth Ranking	**1980s**	**1980s Real GDP per Capita CAGR***	**Nominal GDP per Capita** in 1980**
1	Botswana	10.3%	1181.6
2	Korea	8.4%	1704.47
3	Mongolia	6.8%	—
4	Mauritius	6.0%	1171.58
5	Dominica	5.5%	966.68
6	Hong Kong	5.2%	5700.41
7	Barbados	5.0%	3408.91
8	Laos	4.6%	—
9	Cyprus	4.6%	4232.02
10	Lesotho	4.1%	322
	Average		**2,336**
Growth Ranking	**1990s**	**1990s Real GDP per Capita CAGR***	**Nominal GDP per Capita** in 1990**
1	Equatorial Guinea	17.3%	267
2	Bosnia and Herzegovina	11.5%	—
3	Ireland	8.3%	14,048
4	Kuwait	7.3%	8,795
5	Malta	6.7%	7,192
6	Lebanon	6.2%	1,013
7	Korea	6.1%	6,516
8	Luxembourg	6.1%	34,645
9	Norway	6.1%	28,243
10	Poland	5.9%	1,731
	Average		**11,383**

Growth Ranking	2000s	2000s Real GDP per Capita CAGR*	Nominal GDP per Capita** in 2000
1	Azerbaijan	17.4%	655
2	Angola	14.6%	557
3	Equatorial Guinea	12.6%	1,726
4	Kazakhstan	12.0%	1,229
5	Iraq	11.6%	—
6	Mongolia	10.6%	474
7	Jordan	10.5%	1,652
8	Georgia	9.2%	750
9	Myanmar	9.0%	191
10	Iran	8.9%	1,670
	Average		**989**
Growth Ranking	2010s	2010s Real GDP per Capita CAGR*	Nominal GDP per Capita** in 2010
1	Myanmar	6.1%	979
2	Kyrgyz Rep	6.0%	880
3	Laos	5.3%	1,141
4	Ethiopia	4.7%	342
5	Namibia	4.7%	5,325
6	Mongolia	4.0%	2,643
7	Iraq	4.0%	4,657
8	Lithuania	3.6%	11,985
9	Indonesia	3.6%	3,122
10	Cambodia	3.6%	786
	Average		**3,186**
		Total Average	**3,304**

*Source: Maddison.
**Source: World Bank.

NOTES

On Methodology

For the various GDP growth analyses in the book, I used different data sources depending on the time period I was looking at. For example, if the analysis went back only as far as the 1980s, I tended to use the IMF WEO database, as it is updated twice a year and is standard in academic research. If the analysis looked farther back in time, I tended to use the World Bank data set, which has data back to the 1960s. In examining real per capita growth, which is necessary for work on convergence, I tended to use the Penn World data tables, which have data going back to 1950. For some of the pre-1950 GDP data, I used the Maddison database. Also, throughout the book, figures for debt as a share of GDP are based on data that excludes debts in the financial sector, in order to avoid possible double counting.

Introduction: Impermanence

1. Sujata Rao, "BRIC: Brilliant/Ridiculous Investment Concept," Reuters, December 7, 2011.
2. Harry Wu and Conference Board China Center, "China's Growth and Productivity Performance Debate Revisited—Accounting for China's Sources of Growth with a New Data Set," Economics Program Working Paper Series no. 14-01, January 2014.
3. Andrew Tilton, "Still Wading through 'Great Stagnations,'" Goldman Sachs Global Investment Research, September 17, 2014.
4. Philip E. Tetlock and Dan Gardner, *Superforecasting: The Art and Science of Prediction* (New York: Crown, 2015).
5. Ned Davis, *Ned's Insights*, November 14, 2014.

Chapter 1: Population

1. Charles S. Pearson, *On the Cusp: From Population Boom to Bust* (New York: Oxford University Press, 2015).
2. Rick Gladstone, "India Will Be Most Populous Country Sooner Than Thought," *New York Times*, July 29, 2015.
3. Tristin Hopper, "A History of the Baby Bonus: Tories Now Tout Benefits of Program They Once Axed," *National Post*, July 13, 2015.
4. Nick Parr, "The Baby Bonus Failed to Increase Fertility, but We Should Still Keep It," The Conversation, December 5, 2011.
5. Andrew Mason, "Demographic Transition and Demographic Dividends in Developing and Developed Countries," United Nations, Expert Group Meeting on Social and Economic Implications of Changing Population Age Structures, August 31–September 2, 2005.
6. Christian Gonzales et al., "Fair Play: More Equal Laws Boost Female Labor Force Participation," International Monetary Fund, February 23, 2015.
7. Simone Wajnam, "Demographic Dynamics of Family and Work in Brazil," United Nations, Expert Group Meeting on Changing Population Age Structure and Sustainable Development, October 13–14, 2016.
8. David Rotman, "How Technology Is Destroying Jobs," *MIT Technology Review*, June 12, 2013.
9. John Markoff, "The Next Wave," *Edge*, July 16, 2015.

Chapter 2: Politics

1. Association Thucydide, "Citations sur l'histoire (2/3)," http://www.thucydide .com.

2. Fareed Zakaria, *The Post-American World and the Rise of the Rest* (New York: Norton, 2008).

3. Global Emerging Markets Equity Team, "Tales from the Emerging World: The Myths of Middle-Class Revolution," Morgan Stanley Investment Management, July 16, 2013.

4. "The Quest for Prosperity," *Economist*, May 15, 2007.

5. William Easterly, *The Tyranny of Experts: Economists, Dictators, and the Forgotten Rights of the Poor* (New York: Basic Books, 2014).

Chapter 3: Inequality

1. See, for example, Robert Peston, "Inequality Is Bad for Growth, Says OECD," BBC News, May 21, 2015.

2. Andrew G. Berg and Jonathan Ostry, "Inequality and Unsustainable Growth: Two Sides of the Same Coin," International Monetary Fund, 2011.

3. "Judicial Supervision of Graft Cases Hindering Decision-Making: Arun Jaitley," *Economic Times*, April 27, 2015.

4. Berg and Ostry, "Inequality and Unsustainable Growth."

5. "Global Wealth Report 2014," Credit Suisse, 2014.

Chapter 4: State Power

1. Jonathan Chaat's Compendium of World Wit and Wisdom, https://worldwitandwisdom.com.

2. Ahmed Feteha, "Welcome to Egypt's Fake Weddings: Get High, Leave Lots of Cash," Bloomberg, June 23, 2015.

3. Jong H. Park, "The East Asian Model of Economic Development and Developing Countries," Kennesaw State University, Faculty Publications, December 2002.

4. Ronald Coase and Ning Wang, *How China Became Capitalist* (London: Palgrave Macmillan, 2012).

5. Jun Ma, Audrey Shi, and Shan Lan, "Deregulation and Private Sector Growth," Deutsche Bank Research, September 13, 2013.

Chapter 5: Geography

1. Jonathan Anderson, "How to Think about Emerging Markets (Part 2)," EM Advisors Group, September 4, 2012.

2. Daron Acemoglu, Simon Johnson, and James Robinson, "The Rise of Europe: Atlantic Trade, Institutional Change, and Economic Growth," *American Economic Review* 95, no. 3 (2005): 546–79.

3. S. Kasahara, "The Flying Geese Paradigm: A Critical Study of Its Application

to East Asian Regional Development," United Nations Conference on Trade and Development, Discussion Paper 169, April 2004.

4. Victor Essien, "Regional Trade Agreements in Africa: A Historical and Bibliographic Account of ECOWAS and CEMAC," NYU Global, 2006.

5. Moisés Naím, "The Most Important Alliance You've Never Heard Of," *Atlantic*, February 17, 2014.

6. Ibid.

7. "The World's Shifting Center of Economic Gravity," *Economist*, June 28, 2012.

8. Peter Zeihan, *The Accidental Superpower: The Next Generation of American Preeminence and the Coming Global Disorder* (New York: Twelve, 2014).

9. Sumana Manohar, Hugo Scott-Gall, and Megha Chaturvedi, "Small Dots, Big Picture: Is Trade Set to Fade?" Goldman Sachs Research, September 24, 2015.

Chapter 6: Investment

1. James Manyika et al., "Manufacturing the Future: The Next Era of Global Growth and Innovation," McKinsey Global Institute, November 2012.

2. Louis Gave, "A Better Class of Bubble," Daily Research Note, Gavekal Dragonomics, December 1, 2014.

3. Dani Rodrik, "The Perils of Premature Deindustrialization," Project Syndicate, 2013.

4. Jonathan Anderson, "How to Think about Emerging Markets (Part 2)," EM Advisors Group, September 4, 2012.

5. Ejaz Ghani, William Robert Kerr, and Alex Segura, "Informal Tradables and the Employment Growth of Indian Manufacturing," World Bank Policy Research Working Paper no. WPS7206, March 2, 2015.

6. See, for example, Ejaz Ghani and Stephen O'Connell, "Can Service Be a Growth Escalator in Low-Income Countries?" World Bank, Policy Research Working Paper no. WPS6971, July 1, 2014.

7. Ebrahim Rahbari et al., "Poor Productivity, Poor Data, and Plenty of Polarisation," Citi Research, August 12, 2015.

8. See, for example, Tom Burgis, *The Looting Machine: Warlords, Oligarchs, Corporations, Smugglers, and the Theft of Africa's Wealth* (New York: PublicAffairs, 2015).

Chapter 7: Inflation

1. Helge Berger and Mark Spoerer, "Economic Crises and the European Revolutions of 1848," *Journal of Economic History* 61, no. 2 (June 2001): 293–326.

2. Martin Paldam, "Inflation and Political Instability in Eight Latin American Countries 1946–83," *Public Choice* 52, no. 2 (1987): 143–68.

3. Marc Bellemare, "Rising Food Prices, Food Price Volatility, and Social Unrest," *American Journal of Agricultural Economics* 97, no. 1 (January 2015): 1–21.
4. "World Bank Tackles Food Emergency," BBC News, April 14, 2008.
5. Neil Irwin, "Of Kiwis and Currencies: How a 2% Inflation Target Became Global Economic Gospel," *New York Times*, December 19, 2014.
6. Jim Reid, Nick Burns, and Seb Barker, "Long-Term Asset Return Study: Bonds: The Final Bubble Frontier?" Deutsche Bank Markets Research, September 10, 2014.
7. Irving Fisher, "The Debt Deflation Theory of Great Depression," St. Louis Federal Reserve, n.d.
8. David Hackett Fischer, *The Great Wave: Price Revolutions and the Rhythm of History* (New York: Oxford University Press, 1996).
9. Claudio Borio et al., "The Costs of Deflations: A Historical Perspective," Bank for International Settlements, March 18, 2015.
10. Òscar Jordà, Moritz Schularick, and Alan Taylor, "Leveraged Bubbles," National Bureau of Economic Research, Working Paper no. 21486, August 2015.
11. "Toward Operationalizing Macroprudential Policies: When to Act?" in *Global Financial Stability Report*, chap. 3, International Monetary Fund, September 2011.

Chapter 8: Currency

1. Ed Lowther, "A Short History of the Pound," BBC News, February 14, 2014.
2. Caroline Freund, "Current Account Adjustment in Industrialized Countries," Federal Reserve System, International Finance Discussion Papers no. 692, December 2000.
3. Rudi Dornbusch, interview by *Frontline*, PBS, 1995.
4. Kristin Forbes, "Financial 'Deglobalization'?: Capital Flows, Banks, and the Beatles," Bank of England, 2014.
5. Robert E. Lucas Jr., "Why Doesn't Capital Flow from Rich to Poor Countries?" *American Economic Review* 80, no. 2 (May 1990): 92–96.
6. Paul Davidson, "IMF Chief Says Global Growth Still Too Weak," *USA Today*, April 2, 2014.
7. Oliver Harvey and Robin Winkler, "Dark Matter: The Hidden Capital Flows That Drive G10 Exchange Rates," Deutsche Bank Markets Research, March 6, 2015.

Chapter 9: Debt

1. Claudio Borio and Mathias Drehmann, "Assessing the Risk of Banking Crises—Revisited," *Bank for International Settlements Quarterly Review*, March 2, 2009.

2. "Toward Operationalizing Macroprudential Policies: When to Act?" in *Global Financial Stability Report*, chap. 3, International Monetary Fund, September 2011.

3. The definitive description is in the updated edition of Charles Kindleberger and Robert Z. Aliber, *Manias, Panics, and Crashes: A History of Financial Crises*, 6th ed. (London: Palgrave Macmillan, 2011).

4. Alan M. Taylor, "The Great Leveraging: Five Facts and Five Lessons for Policymakers." Bank for International Settlements, July 2012.

5. Warren Buffett, "Berkshire Hathaway Annual Letter from the Chairman," February 2003, https://berkshirehathaway.com.

6. See, for example, Abdul Abiad, Giovanni Dell'Arrica, and Bin Li, "Creditless Recoveries," International Monetary Fund, 2011.

7. Tim Congdon, "The Debt Threat," *Economic Affairs* 9, no. 2 (January 1989): 42–44.

8. Michael Goldstein, Laura Dix, and Alfredo Pinel, "Post Crisis Blues: The Second Half Improves," Empirical Research Partners, November 2011.

Chapter 10: Hype

1. Barry Hillenbrand, "America in the Mind of Japan," *Time*, February 10, 1992.

2. John F. Copper, *Historical Dictionary of Taiwan (Republic of China)*, 4th ed. (Lanham, MD: Rowman and Littlefield, 2015).

3. Young-lob Chung, *South Korea in the Fast Lane: Economic Development and Capital Formation* (New York: Oxford University Press, 2007).

4. Lant Pritchett and Lawrence Summers, "Asiaphoria Meets Regression to the Mean," National Bureau of Economic Research, Working Paper no. 20573, October 2014.

5. Commission on Growth and Development, "The Growth Report: Strategies for Sustained Growth and Inclusive Development," World Bank, 2008.

6. "Russian President Vladimir Putin Tops Forbes' 2015 Ranking of the World's Most Powerful People," *Forbes*, November 4, 2015.

7. Fernando Gabril Im and David Rosenblatt, "Middle Income Traps a Conceptual and Empirical Survey," World Bank Operations and Strategy Unit, Working Paper no. 6594, September 2013.

8. Pritchett and Summers, "Asiaphoria Meets Regression."

9. Elie Wiesel, *US News and World Report*, October 27, 1986, cited in "Elie Wiesel," Wikiquote.

INDEX

Note: Page numbers in *italics* indicate charts and tables.

ABOUT THE AUTHOR

Ruchir Sharma is head of emerging markets and chief global strategist at Morgan Stanley Investment Management. He travels widely, spending one week every month in a different country, where he meets leading politicians, top CEOs, and other local characters.

Sharma has been a writer for even longer than he has been an investor, and he is a contributing opinion writer at the *New York Times*. Over the past decade he was a frequent contributor to the op-ed pages of the *Wall Street Journal* and the *Financial Times*, and his essays also appeared in *Foreign Affairs, Time, Foreign Policy, Forbes, Bloomberg View*, and other publications. Before 2010 he contributed a regular column to *Newsweek International*.

Sharma's first book, *Breakout Nations: In Pursuit of the Next Economic Miracles*, debuted as the number one bestseller in India, was a *Wall Street Journal* bestseller, and was chosen by *Foreign Policy* as one of its "21 Books to Read in 2012." His 2016 book, *The Rise and Fall of Nations: Forces of Change in the Post-crisis World*, was a *New York Times* bestseller.

Bloomberg named Sharma one of the "Fifty Most Influential" people in the world in October 2015. In 2012, he was selected as one of the "Top Global Thinkers" by *Foreign Policy*; and in June 2013, India's premier weekly magazine, *Outlook*, named him as one of the "World's 25 Smartest Indians." The World Economic Forum in Davos selected Sharma as one of the world's "Young Global Leaders" in 2007.

A committed runner, Sharma competed for India in the sprint relays at a world masters championship and still trains regularly in Central Park.